1 MONTH OF FREE READING

at

www.ForgottenBooks.com

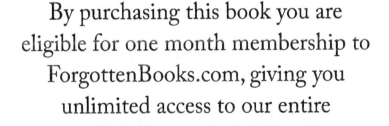

By purchasing this book you are eligible for one month membership to ForgottenBooks.com, giving you unlimited access to our entire collection of over 1,000,000 titles via our web site and mobile apps.

To claim your free month visit:

www.forgottenbooks.com/free893740

ISBN 978-0-266-81576-1
PIBN 10893740

vol. 1

1909.
WEST BROMWICH.
1608-1658.

Staffordshire
Parish Register Society.

EDITOR AND SECRETARY:

REV. F. J. WROTTESLEY,

Denstone Vicarage, Uttoxeter.

=====

DEANERY OF WEST BROMWICH.

West Bromwich Parish Register.

342.46
B4 pr
V. 43

Vol. I.

PRIVATELY PRINTED FOR THE STAFFORDSHIRE PARISH REGISTER SOCIETY.

All Communications respecting the printing and transcription of Registers and the issue of the parts should be addressed to the Editor.

☞ **Attention is especially directed to Notices on inside of Cover.**

The Parish Registers of West Bromwich.

BAPTISMS.

No. 1.   ANNO DOMINI, 1608.   fol. 2.

160⁸⁄₉, Jan.   4.   Jane, d. of Walter Stevens.
,,   Jan.   12.   Elizabeth, d. of Willm. & Mary Stanlye, Gent.

ANNO DOMI., 1609.

1609, Aug.   1.   Margaret, d. of John Dolphin.
1610, Sept.   1.   Marye, d. of Willm. & Mary Stanley, Gent
,,   Sept, 23.   Willm., s. of Symon Warde.
,,   Dec. 10.   Phillip, d. [sic.] of John Edwards.
,,   Dec. 10.   Alice, d. of John Stenleye.
,,   Dec. 10.   Elinor, d. of Adam Barton.

ANNO DOMINI, 1611.

1611, Aug. 18.   Edward, s. of Rychard Dudley.
,,   Sept. 12.   Willm., s. of Rychard White.
,,   Oct.   6.   Margeret, d. of John Partrig.
,,   Oct.   8.   George, s. of John Orris.
,,   Oct. 27.   Elenor, d. of Henry Frith.
,,   Nov.   1.   Allexander, s. of Walter Orris.
,,   Nov. 20.   Ann, d. of Nicholas Ryder.
,,   Dec.   8.   Joyce, d. of John Truelove.
,,   Dec. 19.   Thomas, s. of Willm. James.

Per me, THOMAM JOHNSON,
Ministrum ibidem.

CHRISTENINGES, ANNO DMI., 1611.

1611, Dec. 17.   Mary, d. of Edward Beeby.
,,   Dec. 22.   Elizabeth, d. of John Smith.
,,   Dec. 24.   Ann, d. of Thomas Younge.
,,   Dec. 29.   Ann, d. of Rychard Write.

161½, Jan.   1.   Fraunces, d. of John Street.
   „   Jan. 19.   Alice, d. of Edward Pepwalle.
   „   Jan. 25.   Jane, d. of George Partrig.
   „   Jan. 26.   Robart, s. of John Britle.
   „   Feb.   5.   Frauncis, s. of John Sawnders.
   „   Mar.   1.   Ann, d. of Willm. Turton.
   „   Mar. 22.   Sarai, d. of Willm. Abbot.

Anno Dmi., 1612.

1612, Apr.   2.   Edmund, s. of Nycholas Wylye.
   „   Apr. 10.   Katharine, d. of Rychard Maryan.
   „   Apr. 17.   Robart, s. of Thomas Gretton.
   „   Apr. 26.   William, s. of Willm. Allinn.
   „   May   3.   Elizabeth, d. of Thomas Bickford.
   „   May   9.   Ann, d. of Thomas Blackham.
   „   May   13.   Robart, s. of Raphe Marshe.
   „   May   23.   Alice, d. of John Eaton.
   „   May   29.   Jane, d. of Edward Curtler.
   „   May   30.   Edmund, s. of Edward Morris.
   „   June 20.   George, s. of Edward Fenton.
   „   June 29.   Willm., s. of Ann Attkis, otherwise fls. pop.
   „   July 19.   Frauncis, d. of Roger Smithe.
   „   July 22.   Jone, d. of Henry Hardwick.
   „   Aug. 30.   Rychard, s. of John Gregorye.
   „   Sept. 20.   Marye, d. of the older John Turton, Naylor.
   „   Oct.   3.   Alice, d. of Isahac Hawle.
   „   Oct.   5.   Willm., s. of Edward Robotham.
   „   Oct. 14.   Thomas, s. of John Jesson, Junr.
   „   Oct. 18.   Elizabeth, d. of Roger Collins.
   „   Nov.   1.   Alice, d. of George Underell.
   „   Nov.   2.   Marye, d. of Willm. Wylye.
   „   Nov.   6.   Margeret, d. of Robart Jones.
   „   Nov.   8.   Alice, d. of Symon Croley.
   „   Dec.   4.   Agnes, d. of Willm. Syncoxe.
161⅔, Jan. 28.   John, s. of Symon Warde.
   „   Jan. 31.   Katherine, d. of John Tomlinson.
   „   Feb.   2.   John, s. of Willm. White.
   „   Feb. 22.   Rychard, s. of Rychard Walker.
   „   Feb. 23.   Jone, d. of John Syncoxe.

161⅔, Feb. 23. Jone, d. of Frawncis Cope.
,, Feb. 27. [*omitted*], d. of Edward Cole.
,, Feb. 28. Marye, d. of Rychard Parkes.
,, Feb. 28. Ann, d. of John Ryce *als.* Edwards.
,, Mar. 21. Willm., s. of Rychard Shelfeild.
By me THOMAS JOHNSON.

ANNO DOMI., 1613.

1613, Mar. 25. Frauncis, s. of Thomas Edwards.
,, Mar. 28. Jone, d. of Phillip Tymings.
,, Apr. 5. Jone, d. of Rychard Bird.
,, May 2. George, s. of Rychard Reeve.
,, May 13. Rychard, s. of Umphry Gest.
,, May 20. Elizabeth, d. of John Stanley.
,, May 22. Marye, d. of Michaell Powton.
,, May 27. Francis, s. of [*illegible*].
,, May 30. Rychard, s. of Thomas [*illegible*].
., May George, s. of Edward Willson.
,, June 6. Issabell, d. of John Partrig.
,, June 16. Marye, d. of Thomas Turton.
,, Sept. 6. Fraunces, d. of Symon Bird.
,, Sept. 7. Robart, s. of Robart Ryder.
,, Sept. 19. Adam, s. of Adam Barton.
,, Oct. 10. Symon, s. of Thomas Grettc ..
,, Oct. 30. Mary, d. of Thomas Younge.
,, Nov. 4. Rychard, s. of Willm. Cope.
,, Nov. 7. Margeret, d. of Walter Wylye.
161¾, Jan. 2. Willm., s. of Frauncis Preston, the younger.
,, Jan. 24. Willm., s. of Willm. Eansworth.
,, Jan. 30. Willm., s. of Phillip Clymer.
,, Jan. 30. Alice, d. of John Morris.
,, Feb. 24. John, s. of Roger Smithe.
,, Feb. 24. Elizabeth, d. of Edward Darby.
By me THOMAS JOHNSON.

ANNO DOMI., 1614.

1614, Mar. 27. Mary, d. of Willm. Russell.
,, Apr. 3. Agnes, d. of John Tomlinson
,, Apr. 6. Robart, s. of Robart Bate.

1614, Apr. 18. Elizabeth, d. of Bartholnmewe Moor.
  „   May 31. Ann, d. of Thomas Gibert.
  „   June 24. Frawncis, s. of Walter Orris.
  „   July 3. Marye, d. of Thomas Dudley.
  „   July 3. Willm., s. of Rychard Dudleye.
  „   Aug. 14. Margert, d. of Frauncis Thornton.
  „   Aug. 20. Robart, s. of Willm. Turton.
  „   Aug. 28. Jone, d. of Rychard Marian.
  „   Sept. 4. Elizabeth, d. of John Osborne.
  „   Sept. 25. Agnes, d. of Mychaell Poutney.
  „   Oct. 2. Thomas, s. of Thomas Cashmore.
  „   Oct. 2. Edward, s. of Willm. Carelesse.
  „   Oct. 2. George, s. of Willm. Bissell.
  „   Oct. 9. Ann, d. of John Jesson.
  „   Oct. 10. Ann, d. of John Greslye.
  „   Oct. 10. Jone, d. of George Partrige.

THOMAS JOHNSON.

  „   Oct. 16. Jone, d. of Nycholas Ryder.
  „   Dec. 7. Jone, d. of Edward Morris.
  „   Dec. 11. Jone, d. of Symon Croley.
  „   Dec. 20. Rychard, s. of John Hanson.
  „   Dec. 29. John, s. of Willm. Gremell.
161⅘, Jan. 1. Ann, d. of Gregory Shepherd.
  „   Jan. 1. Elizabeth, d. of Willm. Syncoxe.
  „   Jan. 6. Margery, d. of Edward Cole.
  „   Jan. 9. George, s. of Raphe Marshe.
  „   Feb. 19. Ann, d. of Frauncis Penn.
  „   Feb. 19. Thomas, s. of Thomas Asslin.
  „   Mar. 19. Roger, s. of Roger Smithe.
  „   Mar. 19. Ann, d. of John Turton, Naylor.

THOMAS JOHNSON.

ANNO DOMI., 1615.

1615, Apr. 10. Ann, d. of Nycholas Bridgen.
  „   Apr. 12. Margeret, d. of Roger Collens.
  „   Apr. 16. Margeret, d. of Robart Rider.
  „   May 10. Thomas, s. of Rychard Wilye.
  „   May 17. Marye, d. of Symon Bird.

1615, June 9. Jone, d. of John Ruston.
    ,, June 18. Ann, d. of Robart Jones.
    ,, June 18. Jane, d. of Willm. Wiley.
    ,, June 18. Elizabeth, d. of Izahack Hawle.
    ,, July 20. Willm., s. of Willm. White.
    ,, July 30. Jone, d. of Rychard Parks.
    ,, Aug. 13. Elizabeth, fla. pop.
    ,, Aug. 27. Thomas, s. of John Sawnder.
    ,, Sept. 10. Rychard, s. of Phillipp Clymer.
    ,, Sept. 17. William, s. of George Dugar.
    ,, Sept. 22. Elizabeth, d. of Symon Warde.
    ,, Sept. 28. Elizabeth, d. of Rychard·Henlye.
    ,, Oct. 10. Christophar, s. of John Stonlye.
    ,, Oct. 10. Josephe, s. of Rychard Brake.
    ,, Nov. 5. John, s. of Willm. Cartwrite.
    ,, Nov. 5. Ann, d. of Thomas Gretton.
    ,, Nov. 17. Elizabeth, d. of John Orris.
    ,, Nov. 24. Fraunces, d. of Mychaell Powltney.
    ,, Nov. 24. Elizabeth, d. of Thomas Turton.
    ,, Nov. 24. Alice, d. of Thomas Blackham.
161$\frac{5}{6}$, Jan. 7. John, s. of John Sabine.
    ,, Jan. 7. John, s. of Willm. Coxe.
    ,, Feb. 10. Elizabeth, d. of Rychard Bird.
    ,, Feb. 20. Frauncis, s. of Mr. Wm. Stanley, Esquire,
                   b. Feb. 1.
    ,, Mar. 17. Willm., s. of John Taylor.
    ,, Mar. 17. Rychard, s. of Philip Timings.
    ,, Mar. 17. Elizabeth, d. of Wm. Parrye.
    ,, Mar. 17. Margery, d. of Rychard Write.
    ,, Mar. 24. George, s. of Thomas Younge.

THOMAS JOHNSON.

ANNO DOMI., 1616.

1616, Apr. 5. Frauncis, s. of George Stonley.
    ,, May 18. Ann, d. of Edward Willson.
    ,, May 22. Ann, d. of John Morris.
    ,, July 14. Dorithye, d. of Walter Wylye.
    ,, July 25. Thomas, s. of Willm. Atkis.

1616, Aug. 7.   Thomas, s. of George Sincocks.
  ,, Aug. 19. Edward & Mychaell, ss. of John Sincocks.
  ,, Sept. 7. John, s. of Thomas Stokes.
✓ ,, Oct. 14. Jone, d. of Rychard Write.
  ,, Nov. 1.   John, s. of George Clayton.
  ,, Nov. 10. Jone, d. of Willm. Sincocks.
  ,, Nov. 18. John, s. of Rychard Bett.
  ,, Nov. 17. Margeret, d. of Robart Ryder.
  ,, Dec. 8.   Anne, d. of John Hanson.
  ,, Dec. 27. Anne, d. of Thomas Grove.
  ,, Dec. 28. Willm., s. of Edward Cole.
161$\frac{6}{7}$, Feb. 9. Jone, d. of Edward Pepwell.
  ,, Mar. 2.   Edward, s. of Frauncis Penn.
  ,, Mar. 2.   Margeret, d. of Roger Smithe.
  ,, Mar. 9.   Cicilye, d. of Willm. Johnson.
  ,, Mar. 16. Anne, d. of Thomas Aspling.
  ,, Mar. 16. Sarahe, d. of Thomas Averill.
  ,, Mar. 17. Elizabethe, d. of Willm. Taylor.

THOMAS JOHNSON.

ANNO DOMIN., 1617.

1617, Apr. 1.   Margeret, d. of Peeter Tuncks.
  ,, Apr. 6.   Frauncis, s. of Frauncis Preston.
  ,, Apr. 22. Saincts, d. of John Pice *als.* Edwards.
  ,, May 11. Alice, d. of John Jesson.
  ,, June 9.   Joyce, d. of Roger Collens.
  ,, June 9.   Willm., s. of Willm. Dudleye.
  ,, June 16. Rychard, s. of Raphe Marshe.
  ,, June 16. Willm., s. of Frauncis Thornton.
  ,, June 29. Dorithie, d. of John Partridge.
  ,, July 20. Raphe, s. of Adam Barton.
  ,, Aug. 10. Elizabethe, d. of Gregorye Shepperd.
  ,, Aug. 10. Ann, d. of Henrye Hardwicke.
  ,, Aug. 29. Rychard, s. of Michaell Powtneye.
  ,, Aug. 29. Judithe, d. of Nicholas Hand.
  ,, Sept. 21. Henrye, s. of Robart Bate.
  ,, Oct. 8.   Elnor, d. of Thomas Stokes.
  ,, Nov. 9.   Alice, d. of Phillipp Climer.
  ,, Nov. 16. Ann, d. of Isahack Hawle.

1617, Nov.	19.	John, s. of Nycholas Ryder.
,, Nov.	23.	John, s. of John Granger.
,, Dec.	2.	Ann, d. of Symon Croleye.
,, Dec.	7.	Ann, d. of Willm. Whyte.
,, Dec.	24.	John, s. of Willm. Turton, Junr.
,, Dec.	28.	Jane, d. of Rychard Henleye.
161⅞, Jan.	25.	Mary, d. of Willm. Bissell.
,, Jan.	25.	Elnor, d. of Robart Jones.
,, Jan.	25.	Elizabeth, d. of John Westwood.
,, Jan.	25.	Robart, s. of James Felkin.
,, Jan.	25.	Edward, s. of Willm. Deacon.
,, Jan.	25.	Winifride, d. of George Underill.
,, Feb.	1.	Willm., s. of Willm. Lidiyate.
,, Feb.	1.	Alice, d. of Rychard Parkes.
,, Feb.	7.	George, s. of Rychard Sincox.
,, Feb.	22.	George, s. of John Stonleye.
,, Feb.	29.	Thomas, s. of Thomas Dudleye.
,, Mar.	1.	Ann, d. of John Taylor.
,, Mar.	11.	Alce, d. of John Lambert.

Anno Domini, 1618.

1618, Mar.	29.	Marye, d. of John Osburne.
,, Apr.	6.	Willm., s. of Thomas Hopkis.
,, May	3.	Frauncis, s. of Rychard Bird.
,, May	10.	Willm., s. of Thomas Young.
,, May	19.	Elizabeth, d. of John Newye.
,, June	7.	Marye, d. of Thomas Gilbert.
,, June	24.	Willm., s. of Georg Sincox.
,, June	28.	John, s. of Frauncis Hawcks.
,, July	9.	Ezechiell, s. of Henrye Pateman.
,, July	12.	Willm., s. of Henrye Stonlye.
,, July	25.	John, s. of Willm. Atkis.
,, July	28.	Thomas, s. of Thomas Turton.
,, Aug.	19.	Willm., s. of Thomas Marson.
,, Sept.	20.	Thomas, s. of Willm. Stanleye, Esquire, & buried the same daye.
, Sept.	20.	Jone, d. of John Morris.
,, Sept.	22.	Willm., s. of John Tomlinson.
,, Oct.	4.	Jane, d. of Frauncis Hinkinson.

1618, Oct.	4.	Marye, d. of Willm. Cartwright.
,, Oct.	4.	Elizabeth, d. of John Hanson.
,, Oct.	18.	Dorothye, d. of Rychard Moore.
,, Oct.	29.	Thomas, s. of Rychard Hurbard.
,, Nov.	8.	Rychard, s. of John Owyn.
,, Nov.	8.	Willm., s. of Willm. Round, of Oldberye.
,, Nov.	8.	Marye, d. of John Gadd.
,, Nov.	21.	Ann, d. of Peeter Tunkes.
,, Nov.	22.	Ann, d. of Edward Morris.
161$\frac{8}{9}$, Jan.	10.	Ann, d. of Robart Ryder.
,, Jan.	11.	George, s. of John Jesson.
,, Jan.	24.	George, s. of Walter Wilye.
,, Jan.	24.	Alice, d. of Rychard Dudleye.
,, Jan.	31.	Jone, d. of Roger Smith.
,, Feb.	2.	Thomas, s. of Thomas Grove.

THOMAS JOHNSON.

,, Feb.	7.	Ann, d. of Edward Beebye.
,, Mar.	7.	John, s. of James Felkin.

ANNO DOMINI, 1619.

1619, Mar.	25.	Marye, d. of Georg Clayton.
,, Apr.	9.	George, s. of George Woodward.
,, Apr.	10.	Jane, d. of John Orris.
,, Apr.	14.	Willm., s. of Willm. Coxe.
,, Apr.	21.	Walter, s. of Edward Fenton.
,, Apr.	25.	Ann, d. of Michaell Powltneye.
,, May	18.	Henrye, s. of John Newye.
,, June	6.	Elizabethe, d. of John Partridg.
,, July	25.	Marye, d. of Frauncis Hawckes.
,, July	29.	Elnor, d. of Edward White.
,, Aug.	1.	Jane, d. of John Hawle.
,, Aug.	1.	Mary, d. of Frauncis Penn.
,, Aug.	1.	Elinor, d. of Willm. White.
,, Aug.	15.	Elizabeth, d. of Phillip Climer.
,, Aug.	15.	Jonathan, s. of Willm. Hardwick.
,, Aug.	31.	Frauncis, d. of John Mathewes.
,, Sept.	18.	Jone, d. of Rychard Hurbard.
,, Sept.	19.	John, s. of Willm. Michell.
,, Sept.	19.	Marye, d. of George Syncox.

1619, Sept. 26. Katherin, d. of John Case.
  „   Oct. 17. Frauncis, d. of Willm. Dudleye.
  „   Oct. 24. Mary, d. of John Granger.
  „   Oct. 28. Jone, d. of Thomas Atkis.
  „   Nov. 14. John, s. of Isahack Hawle.
  „   Nov. 21. Frauncis, s. of Frauncis Thornton.
  „   Dec. 12. Marye, d. of Thomas Ember.
  „   Dec. 24. Elizabeth Banner, fla. pop.
16$\frac{19}{20}$, Jan. 2. Jone, d. of John Taylor.
  „   Jan. 30. Thomas, s. of John Gad.
  „   Jan. 30. Jone, d. of Abraham Jobbar.
  „   Feb. 9. Rychard, s. of Rychard Wriht.
  „   Feb. 20. Frauncis, d. of Rychard Henlye.
  „   Feb. 20. Isabell, d. of Willm. Simson.
  „   Mar. 9. Alice, d. of Phillip Timmings.

THOMAS JOHNSON.

  „   Mar. 22. Walter, s. of Walter Wylye.
  „   Mar. 19. Nycholas, s. of Nycholas Hand.

ANNO DOMI., 1620.

1620, Apr. 18. Rychard, s. of Willm. Turton, the younger.
  „   Apr. 23. Jone, d. of Isahack Stanton.
  „   Apr. 29. Thomas, s. of Edward Pepwall.
  „   June 5. John, s. of Willm. Granger.
  „   June 10. Frauncis, s. of John Reeves.
  „   June 17. Marye, d. of Symon Warde.
  „   June 18. Ann, d. of Roger Collins.
  „   July 5. Unica, d. of Thomas Gretton.
  „   July 9. Edwarde, s. of Adam Barton. ✓ 210
  „   July 16. Rychard, s. of Edward White.
  „   July 16. Thomas, s. of Willm. Bissell.
  „   July 21. Henrye, s. of John Partridge.
  „   July 21. Elizabeth, d. of Robart Jones.
  „   Aug. 2. Katherin, d. of Henry Rychards.
  „   Sept. 17. Willm., s. of John Owen.
  „   Oct. 1. Ann, d. of Thomas James.
  „   Oct. 8. Elnor, d. of Thomas Younge.
  „   Oct. 11. Elizabeth, d. of Willm. Deacon.

1620, Oct. 12. Suzanna, d. of Willm. Keeling.
  „   Oct. 13. Willm., s. of Gregorye Shepherd.
  „   Oct. 13. Thomas, s. of Rychard Cowper.
  „   Nov. 12. Walter, s. of Frauncis Preston.
  „   Nov. 12. Nicolas, s. of Robt. Rider.
  „   Nov. 19. Rychard, s. of John Jesson.
  „   Nov. 26. Thomas, s. of Peter Tunkes.
  „   Dec. 17. Frauncis, s. of Rychard Reding.
  „   Dec. 29. Frauncis, d. of John Sabine.
162$\frac{0}{1}$, Jan. 14. Edward, s. of Willm. Atkis.
  „   Feb. 18. Thomas, s. of Michaell Powlton.
  „   Feb. 18. John, s. of John Westwood.
  „   Feb. 24. Thomas, s. of Edward White.
  „   Feb. 28. Ann, d. of Georg Woodward.
  „   Mar. 11. Henrye, s. of Rychard Syncox.

ANNO DOMI., 1621.

1621, Apr. 22. Rychard, s. of Roger Smith.
  „   Apr. 22. Elizabeth, d. of Symon Croley.
                                    THOMAS JOHNSON.
  „   Apr. 28. Anne, d. of Thomas Casmore.
  „   May 3. Margeret, d. of John Woodward.
  „   June 5. John & Willm., ss. of Willm. Hollinsworth.
  „   June 17. Wm., s. of John Newye.
  „   July 18. Susanna, d. of John Stanley *als.* Stonleye
  „   July 28. Ann, d. of Georg Underill.
  „   Aug. 5. Rychard, s. of Rychard Parkes.
  „   Sept. 25. Ann, d. of Thomas Atkis.
  „   Sept. 30. Edward, s. of Edward Morris.
  „   Oct. 7. Thomas, s. of John Tomlinson.
  „   Oct. 14. Michaell, s. of Thomas Turton.
  „   Nov. 25. Jane, d. of Humphrye Gest.
  „   Nov. 25. Elizabeth, d. of James Felkin.
  „   Nov. 25. Thomas, s. of Willm. Hardwicke.
  „   Dec. 12. Sampson, s. of Samuell Gowre, gent.
  „   Dec. 13. Elizabeth, d. of Edward Fenton.
  „   Dec. 16. Thomas, s. of Willm. Cartwright.
  „   Dec. 20. Sara, d. of Isahack Hawle.

162½, Jan. 13. Thomas, s. of Bartholomew Moore.

,,   Jan. 13. Amye, d. of Thomas Grove.

,,   Jan. 13. Jane, d. of John Granger.

,,   Jan. 13. Alice, d. of John Osborne.

,,   Jan. 20. Rychard, s. of Isahack Stanton.

,,   Jan. 20. Dorithye, d. of Raphe Parker.

,,   Mar. 19. [*omitted*], s. of John Westwood.

ANNO DOMI., 1622.

1622, Mar. 19. Alce, d. of John Hanson.

,,   Mar. 29. Henryè, s. of Edward Cole.

,,   Mar. 17. Rychard, s. of Robart Ryder.

,,   Apr. 17. Marye, d. of Willm. Stanley.

,,   Apr. 21. Symon, s. of Walter Vale.

,,   May 26. Susanna, d. of Willm. White.

,,   May 26. Ellin, d. of John Partridge.

,,   June 16. Sara, d. of Thomas Casmore.

,,   July 7. John, s. of John Herd.

,,   July 9. Frauncis, s. of Nicholas Rider.

,,   July 14. Ann, d. of Rychard Henlye.

,,   Aug. 4. Ellen, d. of Nicholas Hand.

,,   Sept. 1. Michaell, s. of Michaell Poulney.

,,   Sept. 8. John, s. of Frauncis Hawkes.

,,   Sept. 15. Marye, d. of Thomas Gilbert.

,,   Oct. 6. Marye, d. of Thomas Emrye.

,,   Dec. 2. Margeret, d. of Rychard Dudleye.

,,   Dec. 22. Thomas, s. of Thomas Stokes.

,,   Dec. 22. Willm., s. of John Hurley.

162⅔, Jan. 1. Caleb, s. of Willm. Russon.

,,   Jan. 1. Martha, d. of Rychard Reding.

,,   Jan. 8. Margery, d. of Willm. Hadleye.

,,   Jan. 19. George, s. of John Owen.

,,   Feb. 2. Thomas, s. of John Pershall.

,,   Feb. 16. Willm., s. of John Jesson.

,,   Mar. 23. Elnor, d. of Peter Tuncks.

ANNO DOMI., 1623.

1623, Mar. 26. John, s. of Ralph Kenrick, Junr.

,,   Mar. 27. [*ómitted*], d. of Robart Jones.

1623, Apr.	9.	Marye, d. of John Hurleye.
,, June	1.	Sarai, d. of George Clayton.
,, June	8.	Marye, d. of Gregory Shepherd.
,, June	15.	George, s. of Roger Smith.
,, June	15.	Thomas, s. of Willm. Michell.
,, June	21.	John, s. of John Chetwin.
,, June	29.	Elizabeth, d. of John Ensworth.
,, July	13.	John, s. of John Newye.
,, July	13.	Thomas, s. of John Hill.
,, July	26.	Dorothye, d. of George Crocket.
,, Sept.	21.	Ellen, d. of Willm. Keeling.
,, Sept.	21.	Marye, d. of Willm. Atkis.
,, Oct.	19.	Henrye, s. of Henrye Hardwicke.
,, Oct.	19.	Thomas, s. of Thomas Reves.
,, Oct.	26.	Nycholas, s. of John Merchurst.
,, Nov.	16.	Willm., s. of Willm. Bird.
,, Nov.	16.	Jone, d. of Georg Aplewis.
,, Nov.	23.	Rychard, s. of Rychard Pargiter.
,, Nov.	30.	Thomas, s. of Thomas Tomlinson.
,, Dec.	7.	Marye, d. of Willm. Russen.
,, Dec.	21.	Thomas, s. of Willm. Hollinsworthe.
162¾, Jan.	18.	John, s. of Thomas Young.
,, Feb.	8.	Margeret, d. of John Bird.
,, Feb.	15.	Amye, d. of Robart Ryder.
,, Feb.	22.	John, s. of Edward White.
,, Mar.	7.	Marye, d. of Willm. Lidyate.
,, Mar.	21.	Izahack, s. of Thomas Hurley.

ANNO DOMI., 1624.

1624, Apr.	25.	Willm., s. of Willm. Osborn.
,, June	10.	Willm., s. of Willm. Partrith.
,, Aug.	22.	John, s. of Water Vale.
,, Sept.	19.	Willm., s. of Willm. Hardwick.
,, Oct.	10.	Daniell, s. of Rychard Jones.
,, Oct.	18.	John, s. of Thomas Atkins.
,, Oct.	19.	Jone, d. of John Granger.
,, Oct.	22.	Elnor, d. of Walter Steven.
,, Oct.	31.	Jone, d. of John Warde.
,, Nov.	9.	Robart, s. of Willm. Jones.

1624, Nov.	25.	Alice, d. of Robart Jomes (Jones).
,, Nov.	28.	Henrye, s. of Rychard Wylye.
,, Nov.	28.	Rychard, s. of John Taylor.
,, Dec.	8.	Ann, d. of John Bedell.
,, Dec.	12.	Izahack, s. of Rychard Weston.
,, Dec.	19.	Jone, d. of Richard Norris.
162⅘, Jan.	2.	Frauncis, s. of John Woodward.
,, Jan.	2.	John, s. of Willm. Preston.
,, Jan.	23.	Robart, s. of Thomas Grove.
,, Jan.	23.	Ann, d. of Willm. Granger.
,, Jan.	30.	John, s. of Michaell Powlton.
,, Jan.	30.	Margeret, d. of Willm. Corbet.
,, Feb.	17.	John, s. of Peeter Tuncks.
,, Feb.	24.	Katherine, d. of Willm. Bird.
,, Feb.	24.	Jane, d. of Robart Ryder.
,, Feb.	24.	Izahack, s. of Roger Smith.
,, Mar.	13.	John, s. of John Partridg.
,, Mar.	20.	Jone, d. of Willm. Hadley.

Anno Domi., 1625.

1625, Apr.	23.	Elizabeth, d. of John Turton, Junr.
,, May	22.	Willm., s. of Nycholas Hands.
,, May	29.	Willm., s. of Thomas Reeves.
,, May	29.	Elizabeth, d. of Edward Browne.
,, June	24.	Katherine, d. of John Jesson.
,, July	17.	Rychard, s. of Willm. James.
,, July	24.	Umphrye, s. of Willm. Dudleye.
,, Aug.	14.	John, s. of John Hawle.
,, Aug.	21.	Elizabeth, d. of Thomas Cashmore.
,, Aug.	28.	Elizabeth, d. of John Ward.
,, Sept.	4.	Elizabeth, d. of Georg Bird.
,, Sept.	17.	Ann, d. of Georg Syncox.
,, Sept.	18.	William, s. of Frauncis Penn.
,, Sept.	25.	Ann, d. of Rychard Hawley.
,, Oct.	2.	Willm., s. of Willm. Syncox.
,, Oct.	2.	Alice, d. of Frauncis Hawkes.
,, Oct.	30.	Frauncis, d. of Raphe Kenrick.
,, Nov.	15.	Edward, s. of Edward Beebye.
,, Nov.	22.	John, s. of John Owyn.

1625, Nov. 22. John, s. of Rychard Gretton.
,,   Nov. 27. Elnor, d. of Rychard Henlye.
,,   Nov. 30. Henry, s. of Thomas Fidoe.
,,   Dec. 27. George, s. of Willm. Paris.
,,   Dec. 28. Jane, d. of Robart Jones.
162$\frac{5}{6}$, Jan. 15. Edward, s. of Edward White.
,,   Jan. 22. Sainctes, d. of Silvester Mathen.
,,   Feb. 1. Henrye, s. of Henrye Newye.
,,   Feb. 2. Rychard, s. of Jeffery Robinson.
,,   Feb. 5. Willm., s. of Frauncis Bird.
,,   Feb. 12. George, s. of John Newye.
,,   Feb. 19. Edward, s. of Willm. Lidiate.
,,   Feb. 23. John & Ann, s. & d. of John Bird.
,,   Feb. 25. Thomas, s. of Walter Steven.
,,   Feb. 25. Josepth, s. of John Taylor.
,,   Feb. 25. Elizabeth, d. of John Tomlinson.
,,   Mar. 19. John, s. of Willm. Osborn.

ANNO DOMINI, 1626.

1626, Apr. 23. Fayth, d. of Thomas Stokes.
,,   May 23. Willm., s. of Willm. Marshe.
,,   May 31. Ann, d. of Georg Peine.
,,   June 11. Robart, s. of John Fluid.
,,   July 23. Henrye, s. of Gregory Shepperd.
,,   Aug. 6. Elizabeth, d. of Willm. Partridg.
,,   Aug. 13. Allexander, s. of Allexander Woodward.
,,   Aug. 13. Ann, d. of Edward Parsons.
,,   Aug. 13. Marye, d. of Rychard Dudleye.
,,   Sept. 10. Ann, d. of Thomas Dutton.
,,   Oct. 1. Edward, s. of Edward Browne.
,,   Oct. 8. Jone, d. of John Tomlinson.
,,   Oct. 8. Ellin, d. of George Plewes.
,,   Oct. 8. John, s. of John Kidson.
,,   Nov. 10. Elizabeth, d. of Thomas Clarke.
,,   Nov. 21. Nicholas, s. of Willm. Preston.
,,   Nov. 29. Ann, d. of Willm. Stanley.
,,   Dec. 3. John, s. of Thomas Heath.
,,   Dec. 3. Elizabeth, d. of Edward Morris.

THOMAS JOHNSON.

1626, Dec.	6.	Henry, illeg. s. of Mary Longam.
,, Dec.	31.	Willm., s. of Willm. Feildust.
,, Dec.	31.	Willm., s. of John Granger.
162$\frac{6}{7}$, Jan.	14.	Raphe, s. of Willm. Hollinsworth.
,, Jan.	16.	Ellin, d. of Nicholas Newye.
,, Jan.	20.	Edwd., s. of Rychard Weston.
,, Feb.	4.	Willm., s. of John Turton, Junr.
,, Feb.	11.	Thomas, s. of Thomas Young.
,, Feb.	11.	Elizabeth, d. of Frauncis Sincox.
,, Feb.	11.	Elizabeth, d. of Izahack Stanton.
,, Feb.	18.	Rychard, s. of John Partridg.
,, Mar.	11.	Nycholas, s. of Michaell Powltney.
,, Mar.	18.	Elnor, d. of Thomas Hurley.
,, Mar.	24.	Sarai, d. of Samuell Seyw.

ANNO DOMINI, 1627.

1627, Mar.	26.	Elizabeth, d. of Willm. Birde.
,, Mar.	28.	Abigaiell, d. of George Clayton.
,, Apr.	8.	Ann, d. of Rychard Reding.
,, Apr.	15.	Willm., s. of George Woodward, Junr.
,, Apr.	29.	Thomas, s. of Henry Frith.
,, May	19.	John, s. of Robart Bate.
,, May	20.	Margeret, d. of Rychard Bird.
,, June	3.	Walter, s. of Walter Vale.
,, June	3.	Katherine, d. of John Chatwin.
,, June	3.	Elizabeth, d. of Willm. Atkis.
,, June	13.	Ann, d. of John Fenton.
,, June	17.	John, s. of Willm. Jones.
,, July	29.	John, s. of Willm. Hadley.
,, Aug.	12.	Elizabeth, d. of John Horton.
,, Aug.	12.	Sarai, d. of Rychard Orris.
,, Aug.	19.	Ellen, d. of Thomas Atkis.
,, Sept.	2.	Marye, d. of John Pershall.
,, Sept.	2.	Willm., s. of Walter Stevens.
,, Sept.	9.	Willm., s. of John Newye.
,, Sept.	23.	Thomas, s. of Thomas Hands.

THOMAS JOHNSON.

| ,, Sept. | 30. | Marye, d. of Willm. Granger. |
| ,, Oct. | 7. | John, s. of Willm. Syncox. |

1627, Oct.   7.   Thomas, s. of John Hindman.
  ,,   Nov.   1.   Ann, d. of Frauncis Atkins.
  ,,   Nov. 11.   John, s. of Willm. Marsh.
  ,,   Dec.   2.   John, s. of John Norris.
  ,,   Dec.   2.   Katherine, d. of Willm. Phillips, b. in par.
                   of Handsworth, but bye licenc of the
                   Minister ther, she was baptized heare.
  ,,   Dec.   9.   Elizabeth, d. of Willm. James.
  ,,   Dec. 16.   Alexander, s. of Frauncis Hawkes.
  ,,   Dec. 16.   Thomas, s. of John Birde.
162⅞, Jan. 20.   John, s. of Thomas Reeves.
  ,,   Jan. 20.   Fraunces, d, of John Warde.
  ,,   Jan. 20.   Ann, d. of Willm. Liddiate.
  ,,   Jan. 20.   Symon, s. of James Ferkin.
  ,,   Feb.   3.   An, d. of Thomas Heathe.
  ,,   Feb. 10.   Henrye, s. of Frauncis Penn.
  ,,   Feb. 10.   Thomas, s. of Raphe Kenrick.
  ,,   Feb. 10.   Marye, d. of John Hawle.
  ,,   Feb. 10.   Margeret, d. of John Westwood.
  ,,   Feb. 17.   Penelope, d. of Rychard Jones.
  ,,   Feb. 29.   Frauncis, s. of Ann Noris, fil. pop.
  ,,   Mar.   2.   John, s. of Willm. Sansom.
  ,,   Mar.   9.   Josepth, s. of Willm. Blackmore.
  ,   Mar.   9.   Willm., s. of Peter Tuncks.
  ,,   Mar. 23.   Frauncis, s. of Henrye Newye.
  ,,   Mar. 23.   Katherine, d. of John Owyn.

Anno Domi., 1628.

1628, Apr. 12.   Alice, d. of Robart Ryder.
  ,,   Apr. 14.   Thomas, s. of Rychard Gretton.
  ,,   Apr. 15.   Jane, d. of Henry Freyth.
  ,,   May   20.   Elizabeth, d. of Edward Parsons.
  ,,   May   27.   Elizabeth, d. of Frauncis Bird.
  ,,   June   8.   Rychard, s. of John Semor.
  ,,   June   8.   Willm., s. of Rychard Henlye.
  ,,   June 15.   Thomas, s. of Frauncis Hinkinson.
  ,,   July   5.   Thomas, s. of Thomas Groves.
  ,,   Aug. 10.   John, s. of Thomas Cashmore.
  ,,   Aug. 17.   Frauncis, s. of Nicholas Newye.

1628, Aug.	17.	Elizabeth, d. of Willm. Dudley.
,, Aug.	24.	John, s. of Thomas Dudley.
,, Aug.	24.	Pricilla, d. of John Hackit.
,, Sept.	7.	Ann, d. of Thomas Fidoe.
,, Sept.	21.	Ann, d. of Edward Deely.
,, Sept.	28.	Jane, d. of John Tomlinson.
,, Oct.	19.	Jane, d. of Henry Basset. ✓
,, Oct.	26.	John, s. of Sawnders Loe.
,, Nov.	2.	Thomas, s. of Rychard Pargiter.
,, Nov.	16.	John, s. of Thomas Hands.
,, Nov.	16.	Christopher, s. of Christopher Okelv
,, Nov.	30.	Marye, d. of John Chelten.
,, Dec.	7.	Thomas, s. of John Case.
,, Dec.	7.	Alice, d. of Rychard Atkis.
,, Dec.	7.	Ann, d. of Henry Bird.
,, Dec.	13.	John, s. of Willm. Durton.
,, Dec.	19.	Thomas, s. of Willm. Bird.
162$\frac{8}{9}$, Jan.	1.	Joseph, s. of John Stumps.
,, Jan.	11.	Marye, d. of Raffe Morris.
,, Jan.	18.	Margery, d. of Willm. Stanley.
,, Jan.	25.	Sara, d. of Willm. Partridg.
,, Feb.	1.	John, s. of Robart Jones.
,, Feb.	1.	Thomas, s. of Thomas Edwards.
,, Feb.	2.	Ann, d. of Frauncis Syncox.
,, Feb.	8.	John, s. of Thomas Stokes.
,, Feb.	8.	Ann, d. of Thomas Dutton.
,, Feb.	15.	Isahacke, s. of Isahacke Stanton.
,, Feb.	15.	Frauncis, d. of Rychard Dudley.
,, Mar.	1.	Katherine, d. of John Horton.

Anno Domi., 1629.

1629, Apr.	4.	Jone, d. of John Granger.
,, Apr.	12.	Elizabeth, d. of Rychard Weston.
,, Apr.	12.	Elizabeth, d. of John Duker.
,, Apr.	14.	Willm., s. of Willm. Turton.
,, Apr.	23.	Thomas, s. of John Semor.
,, May	10.	Sarai, d. of John Bond.
,, May	10.	Ann, d. of Willm. Filldust.
,, May	10.	Alice, d.of Frauncis Green.

1629, May 24. Thomas, s. of Willm. Anderton.

,, June 21. John, s. of Rychard Bird.

,, June 28. Gregory, s. of Gregorye Shepard.

,, July 5. Elizabeth, d. of Willm. Marshe.

,, July 10. Margeret, d. of Edward Diall.

,, July 12. Ann, d. of John Write.

,, July 19. John, s. of John Turton.

,, Aug. 2. Barnabe, s. of Rychard James.

,, Aug. 2. Willm., s. of Robart Bate.

,, Aug. 15. Thomas, s. of Henrye Newye, Junr.

,, Aug. 16. Alice, d. of George *ap* Lewis.

,, Aug. 23. Elizabeth, d. of Rychard Reading.

,, Aug. 30. Thomas, s. of Rychard Traintor.

,, Sept. 13. Alice, d. of Rychard Syncox.

,, Sept. 27. Margeret, d. of John Fenton.

,, Oct. 1. Nycholas, s. of Willm. Carles.

,, Oct. 20. John, s. of John Yardley.

,, Nov. 5. Ann, d. of Gregory Woodward.

,, Nov. 15. Rychard, s. of George Woodward.

,, Nov. 15. Ann, d. of Walter Stevens.

,, Nov. 22. Willm., s. of Willm. Hadleye.

THOMAS JOHNSON.

,, Nov. 22. Ann, d. of John Whithows.

,, Nov. 22. Edward, s. of Elizabeth Brokes, fil. pop.

,, Nov. 29. Iszabell, d. of Willm. Hollinsworth.

,, Dec. 21. Thomas, s. of Elizabeth Langam, fil. pop.

,, Dec. 22. Marye, d. of Willm. Turton.

,, Dec. 22. Elizabeth, d. of Willm. Turton.

16$\frac{29}{30}$, Jan. 6. Allexander, s. of Henry Teye.

,, Jan. 20. Elizabeth, d. of John Warde.

,, Jan. 27. Rychard, s. of John Chetwin.

,, Jan. 27. Thomas, s. of John Partridg.

,, Jan. 27. Edward, s. of Edward Morris.

,, Jan. 27. Jone, d. of Willm. Granger.

,, Feb. 21. Margerye, d. of Rychard Ashmore.

,, Mar. 7. Ann, d. of Thomas Tomlinson.

,, Mar. 20. Mathewe, s. of Mathewe Flecher.

,, Mar. 21. Thomas, s. of Willm. Hadleye.

,, Mar. 21. Iszabell, d. of Edward Parsons, *al.* Lillye.

Anno Domi., 1630.

1630,	Mar.	29.	Iszabell, d. of Henry Frey.
,,	Mar.	30.	John, s. of John Feeld.
,,	Apr.	4.	Iszabell, d. of Thomas Reynolds.
,,	Apr.	11.	Samuell, s. of Lewis Rawley.
,,	Apr.	11.	Amye, d. of Thomas Hurley.
,,	Apr.	11.	Bridget, d. of Matheu Perrye.
,,	Apr.	16.	Iszabell, d. of Iszabell Norris, fla. pop.
,,	Apr.	25.	Willm., s. of Frauncis Johnson.
,,	May	9.	Ann, d. of John Newye.
,,	May	16.	Symon, s. of Thomas Young.
,,	May	16.	Thomas, s. of Robart Jones.
,,	May	16.	Marye, s. of Willm. Lideate.
,,	May	18.	Fayth, d. of Willm. Syncox.
,,	May	18.	Merell, d. of John Norris.
,,	June	8.	Elizabeth, d. of George Rodes.
,,	June	12.	Margeret, d. of Roger Dudell.
,,	June	13.	Izahack, s. of John Hawle.
,,	June	17.	Marye, d. of John Birde.
,,	July	7.	Edward, s. of Edward Tranter.
,,	July	7.	Agnes, d. of Willm. James.
,,	July	9.	Rowland, s. of Rowland Bett.
,,	July	15.	John, s. of John Stamps.
,,	Aug.	8.	Thomas, s. of Walter Vale.
,,	Aug.	29.	Margeret, d. of Raphe Kenricke.
,,	Aug.	29.	Marye, d. of Willm. Partridge.
,,	Sept.	18.	Edward, s. of Edward Diall.
,,	Sept.	21.	George, s. of Thomas Basset. ✓
,,	Sept.	30.	Jone, d. of Edwards Butter.
,,	Oct.	3.	Katherine, d. of Thomas Fidoe.
,,	Oct.	10.	Thamezew, d. of John Case.
,,	Nov.	5.	Joseph, s. of John Bande.
,,	Nov.	7.	Marye, d. of John Duker.
,,	Nov.	14.	Jane, d. of Rychard Pargiter.
,,	Nov.	21.	Raphe, s. of Thomas Churche.
,,	Dec.	5.	Jane, d. of Rychard Tranter.
,,	Dec.	12.	Sarai, d. of Nycholas Newey.
,,	Dec.	19.	John, s. of Willm. Bird.
,,	Dec.	20.	Mary, d. of Willm. Preston.

1630,	Dec.	27.	John, s. of Thomas Heath.
,,	Dec.	28.	Alice, d. of Willm. Stanley.
163⁰⁄₁,	Jan.	9.	Thomas, s. of Henrye Edwards.
,,	Jan.	15.	Willm., s. of Abraham Jesson.
,,	Jan.	16.	Elizabeth, d. of John Bird.
,,	Jan.	16.	Jone, d. of Henry Darby.
,,	Jan.	30.	Thomas, s. of Thomas Atkis.
,,	Feb.	6.	Frauncis, s. of Frauncis Bird.
,,	Feb.	6.	Nycholas, s. of John Wilye.
,,	Feb.	30 (*sic.*).	Thomas, s. of Willm. Jones.
,,	Feb.	29.	Sarai, d. of Thomas Grove.
,,	Feb.	29.	Edward, s. of Rychard Gretton.
,,	Mar.	6.	Margeret, d. of Willm. Marshe.
,,	Mar.	11.	George, s. of George Bird.
,,	Mar.	20.	Joseph, s. of Raphe Morris.
,,	Mar.	20.	[*omitted*], d. of James Firkin.
,,	Mar.	20.	Elnor, d. of Edward Deelye.

Anno Domi., 1631.

1631,	Apr.	3.	Marye, d. of Peeter Tunckes.
,,	Apr.	3.	Phillip, s. of Roger Osborne.
,,	Apr.	12.	John, s. of Rychard James.
,,	Apr.	17.	Adam, s. of Willm. Parkes.
,,	Apr.	24.	John, s. of Rychard Henlye.
,,	Apr.	30.	John, s. of Thomas Clarke.
,,	May	8.	Jone, d. of Thomas Syncox.
,,	May	8.	Marye, d. of Rychard Jones.
,,	May	8.	Marye, d. of John Tomlinson.
,,	May	19.	Ann, d. of Rowland Bett.
,,	May	25.	Iszabell, d. of Margery Hodgkins, fils. pop.
,,	May	29.	John, s. of John Kirtland.
,,	June	5.	Ann, d. of John Chetten.
,,	June	12.	Frauncis, s. of Frauncis Hawkes.
,,	June	19.	Tymothy, s. of Willm. Turton.
,,	June	26.	Ann, d. of Willm. Ward.
,,	July	3.	Marye, d. of Willm. Reeves.
,,	July	17.	Rychard, s. of Thomas Reeves.
,,	July	17.	Edward, s. of Rychard Greensill.
,,	Sept.	15.	Sarai, d. of Frauncis Symcox, of Whisty.

1631, Sept. 26. Elnor, d. of Robart Brisborn.
  „   Sept. 28. Lettis, d. of Robart Shilton, Gent.
  „   Oct.   9. Ann, d. of Thomas Basset.
  „   Oct. 16. Marye, d. of Izaacke Stanton.
  „   Oct. 18. Marye, d. of Willm. Woodward.
  „   Oct. 30. Willm., s. of Christopor Ockley.

                              JOHN BEDENSON.

  „   Oct. 30. Alice, d. of John Granger.
  „   Nov. 20. Jone, d. of Walter Stevens.
  „   Dec.   4. Thomas, s. of Rychard Bird.
163½, Jan. 8. Iszabell, d. of Rychard Partridge.
  „   Jan. 11. John, s. of Frauncis Hodgits.
  „   Jan. 15. Edward, s. of John Feild.
  „   Feb. 12. Rychard, s. of Rychard Dudley.
  „   Feb. 25. John, s. of Willm. Dutton.
  „   Mar.   4. Frauncis, s. of John Partridge.
  „   Mar.   4. Elizabeth, d. of Thomas Tudge.
  „   Mar. 11. Thomas, s. of Willm. Dudley.
  „   Mar. 18. Margeret, d. of Mychaell Powtney.

              ANNO DOMI., 1632.

1632, Apr.   1. Rychard, s. of Rychar Atkis.
  „   Apr. 30. Elizabeth, d. of Edward Tranter.
  „   May   3. John, s. of George Aplowes.
  „   May   13. Alexander, s. of Allexander Loe.
  „   May   22. John, s. of Thomas Dutton.
  „   May   22. Ann, d. of Henry Frith.
  „   May   27. John, s. of Edward Parsons.
  „   June   3. Ann, d. of John Horton.
  „   July   1. Mary, d. of Thomas Reynolds.
  „   July 22. Mary, d. of Henry Edwards.
  „   Aug.   5. Ann, d. of Willm. Sansom.
  „   Aug.   5. Elizabeth, d. of Willm. Hadley.
  „   Aug. 12. Rychard, s. of Edward Hodgkins.
  „   Aug. 19. Nycholas, s. of Willm. Recckard.
  „   Aug. 19. Margert, d. of Rowland Bett.
  „   Aug. 26. Elizabeth, d. of John Wyley.
  „   Aug. 26. Willm., s. of Rychard Reding.
  „   Sept. 9. Thomas, s. of Thomas Mawnton.

1632, Sept. 16.   Elizabeth, d. of John Parsons.
  ,,   Sept. 23.   Allexander, s. of George Woodward.
  ,,   Sept. 30.   Elnor, d. of John Cooke.
  ,,   Oct.   7.   Katherine, d. of Willm. Granger.
  ,,   Oct.   7.   Mary, d. of Willm. Fildust.
  ,,   Oct. 21.   Ann, d. of John Rownde.

WEDDINGS. ANNO DOMI., 1608.

1608, Aug. 16.   Rychard Hopkins & Katherin Haddock.
  ,,   Nov. 22.   Rychard Walker & Frauncis Taylor.
160$\frac{8}{9}$, Jan. 18.   Rychard Russon & Margery Hanson.
1609, Oct. 27.   Symon Warde & Ann Stevens.

In the yeares of our lorde god 1609 & 1610 noe weddings to be found.

ANNO DOMNI., 1611.

1611, Sept. 22.   Greory Sheppard & Mary Parker.
  ,,   Oct.   6.   Edward Morris & Elizabeth Coley.
  ,,   Oct. 20.   Henrye Hardwick & Barbara Briscoe.
  ,,   Oct. 28.   Thomas Briscoe & Elizabeth Sawnders.
  ,,   Oct. 29.   Willm. Sincockes & Elizabeth Hunt.
161$\frac{1}{2}$, Feb.   9.   Willm. Whit & Marye Preston.
1612, Apr. 20.   John Eaton & Alice Syncox.
  ,,   Apr. 21.   John Tomlinson & Margerye Nocke.
  ,,   May   3.   Symon Birde & Jane Hawle.
  ,,   June 14.   John Smith & Elizabeth Savage.
  ,,   June 15.   Mychaell Powton & Mary Sawnders.
  ,,   June 15.   James Allen & Constance Pennye.
  ,,   Sept. 21.   Phillip Clymer & Elizabeth Hand.
  ,,   Sept. 22.   Edward Smith & Mary Partrig.
  ,,   Oct. 20.   John Hanson & Elizabeth Moore.
  ,,   Oct. 25.   Walter Wylye & Margery White.
161$\frac{2}{3}$, Feb.   4.   John Smith & Ann Stokes.

ANNO DOMI., 1613.

1613, Apr.   7.   Thomas Mosse & Ann Myles.

By me THOMAS JOHNSON.

1613, June 28. Edmund Darbye & Jone Hand.
„ Aug. 1. John Biker & Elinor Johnson.
„ Sept. 14. Thomas Cassmore & Jane Westwood.
„ Nov. 7. Thomas Tonge & Jone Syncoxe.
161¾, Feb. 16. Frauncis Penn & Mary Dudley.
„ Feb. 18. Willm. Harrison & Alice Trulove.

By me THOMAS JOHNSON.

ANNO DOMI., 1614.

1614, May 13. Thomas Stanley & Jane Hobbine.
„ May 19. John Sawnders & [*omitted*].
„ June 23. Willm. Cartwright & Margeret Jesson.
„ July 2. John Ruston & Amye Lydyate.
„ July 20. Henry Hardwick & Alice Haththorn.
„ Nov. 1. George Clayton & Marye Edwards.
„ Nov. 9. John Turton & Margaret Darlizon.
„ Nov. 24. George Hunt & Elinor Tuncks, wid.
„ Nov. 26. John Reeves & Winifryde Wheston.

THOMAS JOHNSON.

ANNO DOMINI, 1615.

1615, May 1. Anthonye Scattergood & Joyce Gretton.
„ Sept. 3. Rychard Write & Jone Morris.
„ Oct. 9. Willm. Harris & Alice Harte.
„ Oct. 10. Willm. Atkis & Elizabeth Eynsworthe.
161⅚, Jan. 17. Frauncis Hawks & Marye Jervis.
„ Mar. 16. Thomas Stokes & Elinor Hawle.

THOMAS JOHNSON.

ANNO DOMINI, 1616.

1616, Apr. 22. Willm. Dudleye & Marye Wilye.
„ Apr. 28. Frauncis Hinkinson & Anne Felkin.
„ Nov. 6. Rychard Shedon & Anne Sincocks.
„ Dec. 28. Thomas Stoneye & Margery Wolverston.
„ Dec. 28. Nycholas Hands & Judeth Barnet.
161⁶⁄₇, Jan. 28. John Westwood & Elizabeth Turton.
„ Mar. 3. Arthur Tuncks & Katherin Underill.

THOMAS JOHNSON.

Anno Domini, 1617.

1617, May 12. John Willmore & Elizabeth Sincox.
,, June 3. John Newye & Jone Woodward.
,, Nov. 19. Edward Smith & Elnor Gretton.
161⅞, Jan. 20. John Partridg & Ann Atkis.
,, Jan. 20. Thomas Nicholls & Widow Coaks, of Wednesbury, Lic.

Anno Domini, 1618.

1618, Apr. 28. Thomas Hicks & Elizabeth White.
,, June 25. Thomas Atkis & Mary Stanton.
,, July 26. Edward White & Susanna Smithe.
,, Sept. 13. John Deelye & Jone Norris.
,, Nov. 8. John Tuncks & Elinor Teye.
,, Nov. 30. Thomas Northull & Widdow Underhill.
,, Dec. 9. Symon Leuter & Eme Sheppard, Lic.
161$\frac{8}{9}$, Jan. 18. Robart Felkin & Elinor Marchole.
,, Jan. 26. Willm. Smith & Elinor Harding.
,, Jan. 28. Willm. Michell & Widdowe Bird.

Anno Domini, 1619.

1619, Apr. 29. Isahac Stanton & Dorithye Haddocke.
,, Apr. 29. Thomas Woode & Jane Harper.
,, Sept. 12. Willm. Granger & Ann Hawckes.
,, Oct. 12. Willm. Smith & Marye Stanton.
16$\frac{19}{20}$, Jan. 5. Rychard Cowper & Jane Grove.
,, Feb. 23. Thomas Carelesse & Joyce Weelee.

Anno Domini, 1620.

1620, May 18. Thomas Limes & Elnor Wakelane.
,, June 5. Robart Collins & Ann Rowe.
,, Nov. 15. Frauncis Wiersdall & Elizabeth Hardwick.
,, Nov. 23. Walter Vale & Elnor Haickley.
,, Nov. 30. Willm. Hollinsworth & Ann Langam.
162$\frac{0}{1}$, Jan. 22. Rychard Truelove & Agnes Butter.
,, Jan. 31. Edward Fones & Ann Okell.

Anno Domini, 1621.

1621, June	4.	George Lewis & Alice Gill.	
,, June	12.	Charles Green & Unica Holland.	
,, June	15.	Nicholas Kilbe & Marget Wiersdale.	
,, July	18.	Roger Smith & Joyce Arrowsmith.	
,, Aug.	6.	George Bird & Elizabeth Hearinge.	
,, Nov.	20.	Willm. Preston & Florence Orme.	
162½, Jan.	16.	Willm. Russon & Jone Huse.	
,, Feb.	18.	George Clayton & Jone Somerland.	

Anno Domi., 1622.

1622, May	13.	Willm. Johnson & Jone Frecleton.	
,, May	23.	George Croket & Frauncis Granger.	
,, May	23.	Adam Barton & [*omitted*] Heath.	✓ 20 5
,, June	22.	Thomas Reeves & Ann Jesson.	
,, Oct.	7.	Edward Tapping & Margeret Smith.	
,, Oct.	23.	John Asleye & Ann Asleye.	

Anno Domni., 1623.

1623, May	1.	John Reynolds & Marye Jones.
,, June 29.		Willm. Partridg & Elizabeth Basege.
,, Aug.	3.	Willm. Woodward & Jone Russon.
,, Sept.	28.	John Timings & Jone Gest.
,, Sept.	29.	Thomas Parker & Elizabeth Sheldon.
,, Sept.	29.	Barnard Ludman & Bethice Rowe.
,, Sept.	13.	John Lillye & Jone Hobbins.
,, Nov.	1.	John Beedle & Sarai Waren.
,, Nov.	27.	Gregorye Haddock & Margeret White.
162¾, Jan.	19.	Thomas Langston & Elnor Corns.
,, Jan.	21.	John Banister & Ann Holland.
,, Jan.	21.	Rychard Jones & Marye Atkes.
,, Jan.	25.	Rychard Silvester & Marye Tunks.
,, Jan.	28.	Water Steevens & Iszabell Wolverstone.

Anno Domi., 1624.

1624, July	5.	Steven Warde & Winifrid Sincox.
,, Nov.	29.	Willm. Jones & Ann Litley.
,, Nov.	29.	Frauncis Hodgets & Iszabell Johnson.

1624, Nov. 12.　Rychard Hawkesford & Iszabell Partridg.
162⅘, Jan. 16.　Edward Hopkins & Elizabeth Richards, Wid.
„　Jan. 16.　Rychard Bird & Margert Marshe.
„　Feb. 21.　Henry Hunt & Em Colye.
„　Feb. 29.　Edward Bancks & Katherine Wells.

Anno Domi., 1625.

1625, May 8.　Willm. Sansom & Margeret Teye.
„　May 11.　John Bird & Ann Partridg.
„　Aug. 16.　Gregorye Woodward & Ann Downing.
„　Oct. 12.　Thomas Heelye & Thamezin Cowper.
„　Oct. 23.　Allxander Woodward & Margert Loe.
„　Oct. 30.　John Sincox & Elnor Ferkin.
„　Nov. 7.　Bezahell Ringht & Elizabeth Turton.
162⅚, Feb. 6.　Edward Morris & Joyce Hodgkins.

Anno Domini, 1626.

1626, July 23.　Henrye Free & Alice Carelesse.
„　Sept. 4.　John Stanton & Mary Bird, Wid.
„　Sept. 17.　John Horton & Elizabeth Hayward.
„　Oct. 22.　Willm. Hadley & Joyce Ocklye.
162⁶⁄₇, Jan. 16.　Edward Beebye & Ann Partridg, wid.

Anno Domini, 1627.

1627, May 27.　Willm. Blackmor & Winifride Dolphin.
„　June 19.　Thomas Davis & Elnor Stevens.
„　June 30.　Thomas Fetherstone & Ann Bruerton, Wid.
„　Sept. 9.　Thomas Clarke & Ann Tarrye.
„　Oct. 16.　Rychard Atkins & Alice Hardwick, Wid.
„　Oct. 28.　Christopher Okelye & Ellen Hides.

Anno Dmi., 1628.

1628, June 9.　John Yardley & Elnor Sincox.
„　June 21.　John Pinion & Margery Nelson.
„　June 21.　John Duker & Alice Orris.
„　June 30.　Frauncis Green & Margeret Careles.
„　July 13.　John Wright & Katherin Leayd.
„　July 30.　Symon Reade & Alice Briscoe.

1628, Oct.   7. John Bond & Iszabell Wilson.
   ,,   Oct. 19. Rychard Trainter & Mary Cutler.
162⁸⁄₉, Jan. ´26. Roger Wright & Ann Costeloe.   ✓
   ,,   Jan. 27. John Dolphin & Elizabeth Syncox.

ANNO DOMNI., 1629.

1629, May   26. Thomas Reinolds & Mary Allèn.
   ,,   July 13. Frauncis Johnson & Iszabell Jesson.
   ,,   Aug. 18. John Derrick & Ann Chessher.
   ,,   Sept. 13. John Deelye & Margeret Deelye.
   ,,   Sept. 20. Rowland Bett & Ann Shropshere.
   ,,   Oct. 25. Edwarde Dudley & Marye Powtney.
   ,,   Nov.   8. John Wylye & Elizabeth Wawker.
   ,,   Nov. 30. John Sadler & Marye Botte.
16²⁹⁄₃₆, Jan. 18. Willm. Atton & Agnes Morris.
   ,,   Jan. 21. Edwarde Reynolds & Elizabeth Brokes. ✓ ❨

ANNO DOMI., 1630.

1630, Apr. 26. Henrye Edwards & Elnor Stanton.
   ,,   June 13. Edward Daye & Fraunces Okeley.
   ,,   June 20. Henrye Wright & Sarai Colte.   ✓
   ,,   Aug.   1. Thomas Syncox & Jane Careles.
   ,,   Aug.   2. Edwarde Tranter & Ann Cutler.
   ,,   Aug. 10. Thomas Churche & Margeret Marshe.
   ,,   Aug. 24. Hewghe Nycholas & Elizabeth Cole.
   ,,   Dec. 15. John Stevens & Elizabeth Dolphin.
163⁰⁄₁, Jan. 18. John Taylor & Iszabell Herring.
   ,,   Jan. 31. Rychard Greensell & Ann Osborne.
   ,,   Feb. 14. John Gibson & Jone Cole.

ANNO DOMI., 1631.

1631, May   16. Walter Stevens, Junr., & Elizabeth Green. ✓ ꜛ
   ,,   June 12. Edward Sharpling & Iszabèll Grice.
   ,,   Sept. 11. John Syncox & Elizabeth Bodelye.
   ,,   Oct. 27. Edward Hodgkins & Màrye Keeling.
163½, Jan. 26. Edward Cole & Jone Perry.
   ,,   Feb. 12. Thomas Grove & Amye Jesson.

Anno Domi., 1632.

1632, May 21. Edward Grove & Ann Dudley.
,, May 22. Elias Darom & Ann Young.
,, July 2. John Parsons & Joyce Stokes.
,, Oct. 24. Willm. Rychards & Elizabeth Jervis.
,, Nov. 20. Thomas Asplew & Alice Syncox.
163⅔, Feb. 25. John Wolvestone & Mary Turton.

Anno Domi., 1633.

1633, Apr. 22. Willm. Rychards & Fraunces Done.
,, July 16. John Hilton & Elizabeth Syncox.
,, July 23. Thomas Blackham & Elnor Heath.
,, Oct. 21. Thomas Frith & Mary Grise.
,, Nov. 2. Phillip Ensworth & [*omitted*] Bird.

Anno Domi., 1634.

1634, Apr. 14. Willm. Parks & Em Hardwick.
,, July 3. Willm. Grice & Ann Deely.
,, July 14. Rychard Orris & Elizabeth Welch.
,, July 27. George Syncox & Joyce Trulove.
,, Sept. 2. John Haslock & Jone Chesheir.

Anno Domi., 1635.

1635, May 1. Willm. Chetwin & Elizabeth Edwards.
,, July 14. John Baker & Alce Hall.
,, July 16. Thomas Briskow & Alce Staunton.
,, July 30. Raphe Watton & Judethe Hancoxe.
,, Aug. 9. George Stot & Amy Wiersdale.
,, Aug. 15. Willm. Hopley & Elizabeth Westwood.
,, Aug. 17. Thomas Ball & Sarah Partrich.
,, Aug. 17. Willm. Hogets & Jone Tudge.
,, Aug. 24. George Parboe & Ann Shepard.
,, Oct. 19. Willm. Allin & Elizabeth Deely.
,, Nov. 4. Mr. Thomas Johnson & Maudlin Sibles.
,, Nov. 17. John Colman & Ann Record.
163⅚, Jan. 7. George Paint & Ann Bridgin.
,, Jan. 14. John Stanly & Elizabeth Smith.
,, Feb. 4. Michaell Perey & Jane Knoles.
,, Feb. 18. John Cadwalladar Jones & Alce Buxton.

Anno Domi., 1636.

1636, Apr. 28. Thomas Cope & Elizabeth Sincox.
,, June 14. Thomas Underhill & Elizabeth Marshe.
,, July 5. George Addams & Margery Stony.
,, July 12. Willm. Perkin & Frauncis Tomlinson *al.* Browne.
,, Aug. 29. Henry Wasse & Katheren Salt.
,, Oct. 18. Edward Dudley & Anne Cartwright.

THOMAS GROVE, }
JOHN BIRD, } Economis.

Anno Domi., 1637.

1637, May 2. Willm. Chambers & Mary Dudley.
,, Nov. 7. Robert Marsh & Anne Dudley.
,, Nov. 9. Frauncis Poulton & Elizabeth Endsor.
,, Nov. 27. George Basset & Alice Greene.
,, Nov. 26. Thomas Wiersdale & Elizabeth Salt.
,, Nov. 28. Henry Knight & Jane Meanek.
163⅞, Jan. 16. William Winter & Iszabell Sharpling.
,, Jan. 18. John Bird & Mary Young.
,, Jan. 21. George Bines & Alice Careles.

THOMAS JESSON,
WILLM. STERRY, Economis.

Anno Dom,. 1638.

1638, Apr. 28. Willm. Allen & Maudlin Johnson.
,, June 12. Willm. Wall & Ellonar Frith.
,, Aug. 13. John Edwards & Elizabeth Costiloe.
,, Oct. 20. Henry Edwards & Jone Clarkeson.
,, Nov. 1. Edward Mordick & Anne Sault.
,, Nov. 5. John Rider & Ellonar Piggott.

Anno Dmi., 1639.

1639, May 15. Robert Blakesley & Susanna Rawley.
,, May 17. Richard Hanson & Lucy Hadley.
,, June 2. William Hames & Ales Thorton.
,, July 28. William Gilbart & Margaret James *alias* Stringer.

1639, June	24.	Hugh Merrihurst & Elizabeth Duker.
,, Aug.	26.	William Ebbe & Jane Partrich.
,, Sept.	9.	Robert Haywood & Ciciley Bennet.
,, Sept.	17.	Thomas Gilbard & Mary James.
,, Sept.	23.	William White & Isabell Norris.
,, Nov.	3.	Water Wiley & Margery Gibbens.
,, Oct.	17.	William Shelfield & Elizabeth Stanley.
,, Oct.	29.	George Basett & Mary Cartwright.
16$\frac{39}{40}$, Jan.	19.	Edmund Dixon & Ellonar Tymins.
,, Jan.	20.	Robert Turner & Alice Peppall.

Anno Dmi., 1640.

1640, Apr.	21.	John Marson & Frances Bartlett.
,, June	2.	William Wyley & Anne Hall.
,, May	26.	Hughe Wooddman & Dorothy Hickman.
,, July	9.	John Ward & Ellonar Partrich.
,, Aug.	24.	Richard Wheeler & Margery Reeve.
,, Aug.	31.	John More & Ann Hall.
,, Sept.	15.	Richard James & Isabell Hall.
,, Sept.	21.	John Dimunt & Margarett Wyley.
,, Nov.	8.	John Baker & Anne Jesson.
,, Nov.	11.	John Beetmyson & Winifred Underhill.
,, Nov.	17.	Edward Curtler & Francis Allen.
164$\frac{0}{1}$, Feb.	14.	Henry Bate & Anne Ensworth.
,, Feb.	16.	Michaell Sincox & Elizabeth Hewey.
,, Feb.	20.	William Taylor & Mary Phillips.
,, Feb.	21.	Thomas Atkins & Mary Wall.

Anno Dni., 1641.

1641, May	4.	Robert Merrihurst & Mary Beebye.
,, May	9.	Henry Avrill & Mary Wyley.
,, May	11.	William Penney & Elizabeth Brooks.
,, July	6.	Robert Gretton & Elizabeth Turton.
,, Aug.	29.	George Robhurst & Mary Henley.
164$\frac{1}{2}$, Jan.	25.	William Blakemore & Ann Beebie.
,, Jan.	30.	John Acherley & Margert Aston.
,, Feb.	2.	Raph Stanley & Katherine Rasson.
,, Feb.	4.	Thomas Reede & Alice Dudley.

1642.

1642, Apr.	3.	John Salt & Katherine Case.	
,, May	30.	Richard Darby & Mary Reard.	
,, July	3.	William Lydyate & Ellonar Yong.	
,, Aug.	15.	Walter Wyley & Mary Brisome.	
,, Sept.	5.	James Evans & Ann Morris.	
,, Sept.	21.	Robert Turner & Ann Jones.	
,, Sept.	26.	John Cole & Jone Wright.	✓
,, Nov.	2.	Thomas Hurly & Jone Taylor.	
,, Nov.	22.	John Jewen & Jone Ellice.	
,, Nov.	28.	Richard Salt & Elizabeth Jones.	
,, Nov.	28.	Water Fenton & Elizabeth Croley.	
164⅔, Feb.	6.	George Millard & Anne Grice.	
,, Feb.	13.	William Parks & Anne Blackham.	

1643.

1643, May	13.	Edward Birch & Ann Jesson.	
,, June	9.	Richard Carles & Elizabeth Hall.	✓ 9
,, June	9.	John Upton & Sibbell Sutton.	
,, June	6.	Roger Shenton & Frances Granger.	
,, June	13.	George Jesson & Mary Ford.	
,, July	3.	John Guy & Marian Edwards.	
,, Aug.	8.	Willm. Osborne & Dorothy Wyley.	
,, Dec.	27.	Willm. Warram & Joyce Taylor.	
164¾, Feb.	6.	Thomas Cashmore & Jone Siddowne.	

1644.

1644, July	9.	William Whit & Kathren Hurlbut.	
,, Sept.	1.	John Hall & Ann Pargeter.	✓ 100
,, Dec.	3.	Isacke Dutton & Ann Smallwood.	
164⅘, Jan.	28.	Thomas Tunckes & Marye Hurlbut.	

1645.

1645, May	6.	Samuell Higgins & Ann Birges.	
164⅚, Jan.	31.	Edward Birges & Dorothy Martin.	

1646.

1646, June	9.	John Stamps & Ann Granger.	
,, Nov.	10.	Hendry Leese & Ann Prise.	

1646, Dec. 21.   John Bird & Ann Kirtland.
164⁶⁄₇, Jan. 19.   John Lester & Margery Birges.

1649.

1649, June 21.   Robart Turton & Mrs. Sara Shelton.
  ,,   July 9.   Edward Dudley & Sara Willets.
  ,,   Aug. 13.   William Gettell & Alce Jesson.
  ,,   Aug. 25.   Zackary Juckes & Jone Michell, of Birming-
                  ham.

BURIALLS.   1608.

1608, Aug. 10.   Agnes, w. of Rychard Asley.
  ,,   Sept. 30.   Alice, w. of Thomas Hadley.

1609.

1609, Aug. 1.   Joyce, w. of Richard Asley, the younger.

1610.

1610.   Ther are none fownde to be buryed.

1611.

1611, Aug. 7.   Ann, d. of John Orris.
  ,,   Sept. 29.   Jone, w. of James Owyn.
  ,,   Nov. 10.   Cycelye Walton.
  ,,   Nov. 10.   Elizabeth Trey.
161½, Feb. 26.   Brydget Darbye.
  ,,   Feb. 27.   Walter Cornfort, a stranger.
  ,,   Mar. 12.   Rychard Stanley, Gent.
  ,,   Mar. 24.   Elizabeth Atkis.
                  By me THOMAS JOHNSON.

ANNO DOMI., 1612.

1612, May 12.   Elizabeth, d. of Willm. Stanley, gent.
  ,,   May 18.   Ann Winsmore.
  ,,   May 25.   Robart Rychards.
  ,,   June 26.   Alice, d. of John Eaton.
  ,,   July 1.   Thomas Browne.

1612, July 27. Barbara, w. of Henry Hardwicke.
  ,,   Aug. 31. Roger Bennet.
  ,,   Oct.   1. Jone Birde.
  ,,   Nov. 10. Elizabeth, w. of John Turton, the younger,
                   Naylor.

                            THOMAS JOHNSON.

  ,,   Nov. 25. Margaret, d. of Bartholomew Moore.
  ,,   Nov. 26. Iszabell Redale.
  ,,   Dec. 29. Willm. Parkes had a sonne buried before
                   baptisme.
161⅔, Jan. 16. Ann, d. of Henry Hardwick.
  ,,   Jan. 18. Elizabeth Mosse.
  ,,   Jan. 20. Thomas Dudley had a sonne buryed, dying
                   before baptisme.
  ,,   Jan. 22. Elizabeth, d. of Nycholas Persall.
  ,,   Feb.   4. Ann Williams.

                        1613.

1613, Apr. 11. Elizabeth, w. of Christophor Penn.
  ,,   Apr. 13. Rychard Rushan.
  ,,   June 10. Ann, d. of Thomas Gibert.
  ,,   July 21. Robart Hawle.
  ,,   Aug.   3. Winifride, w. of John Dutton.
  ,,   Aug. 24. Willm. Cole.
  ,,   Sept. 4. Ann Westwood.
  ,,   Sept. 12. Jone Westwood.
√ ,,   Oct.   4. Adam, s. of Adam Barton.   20 7
  ,,   Oct.   6. Elizabeth Bickford.
  ,,   Oct. 15. John Watt.
  ,,   Nov.   4. Iszabell Butler.
  ,,   Dec. 19. Thomas Hindes.
  ,,   Dec. 26. Lawrence Peerson.
161¾, Jan.   3. Frauncis Ammersleye.
  ,,   Jan.   9. Thomas Truelove.
  ,,   Feb.   1. Raphe Stanley.
  ,,   Feb.   9. Thomas James.
  ,,   Feb. 12. Alice Hand.
  ,,   Feb. 13. George Rychards.

161¾, Feb. 24. Willm. Eansworth.
,, Feb. 28. Mary Okelye.
,, Mar. 4. Elizabeth Eady.
,, Mar. 11. Edmund Bird.
,, Mar. 11. John, s. of Roger Smith.
,, Mar. 12. Elizabeth Maddocke.

Anno Domi., 1614.

1614, Apr. 15. Jone Jesson.
,, Apr. 18. Nycholas Murrin.

THOMAS JOHNSON.

,, June 29. Elizabeth, d. of [omitted] Deacon of Churleye.
,, July 17. Rychard Reeves.
,, Aug. 21. Willm. Whorwood, Knight.
,, Aug. 22. Ann, d. of John Tomlinson.
,, Sept. 4. Jone Woode.
,, Oct. 23. Robart, s. of Robart Ryder.
,, Oct. 27. Elizabeth Johnson.
,, Nov. 4. Rychard, s. of Frauncis Ashmore.
,, Nov. 8. Willm., s. of Rychard Dudley.
,, Nov. 10. Margert, d. of John Dolphin.
,, Nov. 19. Willm., s. of Frauncis Green.
,, Nov. 20. Frauncis Woode.
,, Nov. 20. Edward, s. of Edward Morris.
,, Dec. 1. John, s. of John Einsworth.
,, Dec. 2. Sarai Haicley.
,, Dec. 11. Thomas Bradley.
,, Dec. 25. Jone, d. of Edward Beeby.
,, Dec. 28. Nicholas, s. of Nicholas Saunders.
161⅘, Jan. 2. Rychard, s. of Thomas Hemings.
,, Jan. 13. Thomas Farley.
,, Jan. 25. Mark Clarke.

THOMAS JOHNSON.

,, Feb. 10. Rychard Belche.
,, Feb. 20. [*omitted*], w. of Willm. Cole.
,, Feb. 21. Amye, d. of John Taylor.
,, Mar. 8. Elizabeth Birch, Wid.
,, Mar. 19. Thomas Cradley.

THOMAS JOHNSON.

ANNO DOMI., 1615.

1615,	Apr.	10.	Walter Stanley, Esquire.
,,	May	10.	Roger Turnleye.
,,	June	7.	Frauncis, s. of Walter Orris.
,,	June	9.	Rychard, s. of James Allen.
,,	June	25.	John, s. of Roger Collins.
,,	July	13.	Alice, wid. of John Watt.
,,	July	19.	John Jesson, thelder.
,,	Aug.	8.	The Stranger that died at John Sabins.
,,	Sept.	16.	Winifride, d. of Nicholas Jesson.
,,	Oct.	7.	Nicholas Blackham, a Stranger.
,,	Oct.	8.	Robart Dawe.
,,	Oct.	20.	Kathrin, w. of John Partridge.
,,	Nov.	8.	Dorothye Rychards, wid.
,,	Dec.	18.	Henrye, s. of John Jesson.
,,	Dec.	21.	Edward, s. of John Morris, the younger.
161$\frac{5}{6}$,	Jan.	1.	Margery, w. of John Curtler.
,,	Jan.	1.	John Boomer.
,,	Jan.	14.	Alice, w. of John Hawks.
,,	Jan.	27.	Elizabeth, w. of Thomas Partridg.
,,	Feb.	10.	Willm. Cox.
,,	Feb.	15.	Robart Aston.
,,	Feb.	23.	Elizabeth Fresons, wid.
,,	Feb.	27.	Jone Aspling, wid.
,,	Feb.	30 (*sic.*).	Dorothy Bacon.
,,	Mar.	7.	Alice Hill, wid.
,,	Mar.	12.	George, s. of Willm. Yardley.
,,	Mar.	17.	Thomas Partridge.
,,	Mar.	17.	Jane Crocket, wid.

ANNO DOMINI, 1616.

1616,	Mar.	28.	Willm., s. of Willm. Yardley.
,,	Apr.	6.	Jone Bowers, wid.
,,	Apr.	8.	Elizabeth Bennet, wid.
,,	Apr.	17.	Winifryd, d. of Edward Rowbottom.
,,	May	12.	Thomas Williamson.
,,	May	18.	Willm. Fowke.
,,	May	25.	John Turton.

1616, May 26.   Elnor Rowbottom.
  ,,   July 23.   Alice, w. of Robart Felkin.
  ,,   Sept. 10.   Ellen, w. of Nycholas Hands.
  ,,   Sept. 20.   John, s. of Thomas Stockes.
  ,,   Nov. 3.   Jone Hopkis, wid.
161$\frac{6}{7}$, Jan. 1.   Jone, w. of Raphe Tuncks.
  ,,   Jan. 17.   Robart Middlemore, gent.

THOMAS JOHNSON.

ANNO DOMINI, 1617.

1617, Apr. 3.   Jane, w. of Thomas Edwards.
  ,,   May 17.   Machin, s. of Eedye Wylye.
  ,,   Nov. 2.   Ann Williamson, wid.
  ,,   Nov. 5.   Symon Bird.
161$\frac{7}{8}$, Jan. 6.   John, s. of Symon Bird, deceased.
  ,,   Jan. 13.   William, s. of Symon Bird, deceased.
  ,,   Feb. 23.   John White.
  ,,   Mar. 2.   Elizabeth Shelton.
  ,,   Mar. 10.   John Osborne.

ANNO DOMI., 1618.

1618, May 12.   John Young.
  ,,   May 30.   Jone, w. of John Young.
  ,,   July 3.   Durphrey Filke's Wife.
  ,,   July 29.   Willm. Hawle.
  ,,   July 30.   John, s. of Frauncis Hawckes.
  ,,   Aug. 26.   Elizabeth Lidiate.
  ,,   Aug. 27.   Edward, s. of Rychard Henley.
  ,,   Sept. 7.   Willm. Keeling.
  ,,   Sept. 15.   Widdow Kinder.
  ,,   Nov. 3.   Thomas, s. of Rychard Hurbert.
  ,,   Nov. 24.   Mrs. Underwood, wid.
  ,,   Dec. 16.   Willm., s. of George Syncox.
  ,,   Dec. 29.   Ann, w. of Thomas Carelesse.
161$\frac{8}{9}$, Jan. 17.   Ann, w. of Thomas Wood.
  ,,   Jan. 2.   Elizabeth, w. of Willm. Syncox.
  ,,   Feb. 21.   Edward, s. of Willm. Deacon.
  ,,   Mar. 15.   George, s. of Walter Wylye.

Anno Domi., 1619.

1619, May 2. Ann Gresleye.
   „   June 3. Ann, d. of Adam Barton. ✓ 20 6
   „   June 3. Elinor, d. of Edward White.
   „   June 14. Mawde Langham, wid.
   „   July 24. Margery, w. of John Dolphin.
   „   Oct.   6. Frauncis Kinder.
   „   Oct. 10. Thomas Heemings.
   „   Oct. 28. Frauncis, w. of Willm. Allen.
   „   Nov. 29. Jone, d. of Thomas Atkis.
16$\frac{19}{20}$, Feb. 28. Jhone Heaving.
   „   Mar.   9. Frauncis, s. of Umphry Gest.
   „   Mar. 14. John Dutton.

Anno Domi., 1620.

1620, Mar. 28. Richard Piddock.
   „   May 21. Thomas Briscoe.
   „   June 16. Jone & Frauncis, ds. of Symon Crolye.
   „   June 26. Alice Felkin.
   „   July   1. Jone, d. of John Noris.
   „   Aug.   3. Sara, d. of Wid. Baker.
   „   Aug.   5. Margeret, w. of Adam Barton. ✓ 20 21
   „   Nov.   4. The d. of Rychar Eayre.
   „   Nov.   4. The s. of John Tomlinson.
   „   Nov. 14. Willm. Wood.
   „   Nov. 17. Jone Fowlke.
   „   Nov. 18. Rychard Rowe.
   „   Nov. 28. Widowe Wilye.
   „   Nov. 29. The w. of Robart Bates.
162$\frac{0}{1}$, Jan. 1. Edward, s. of Adam Barton. ✓ 21 0
   „   Jan. 14. John Wiersdale.
   „   Jan. 22. Frauncis Preston.
   „   Jan. 25. John Haickleye.
   „   Jan. 27. Widowe Howghe.
   „   Jan. 27. Elnor, d. of Willm. White.
   „   Mar.   7. Thomas Partridg.
   „   Mar. 23. Thomas, s. of Rychard Cowper.

ANNO DOMI., 1621.

1621, Apr. 20. Rychard Asleye.
,, May   1. Marye, w. of Georg Clayton.
,, May   3. Dorithe, d. of Thomas Casmore.
,, May 20. Roger, s. of Robart Heywood.
,, June 10. John, s. of John Westwood.
,, June 24. Widow Osborn.
,, July 8. Frauncis Lane.
,, July 27. George White.
,, Aug. 27. Rychard Wains, Gent.
,, Aug. 28. Nycholas Wilee.
,, Sept. 9. Winifrid, w. of John Reeves.
,, Dec. 10. Allexander Atkis.

THOMAS JOHNSON.

,, Dec. 10. Willm. Bird.
,, Dec. 12. Widow Hanson.
162½, Jan.   2. Marye, d. of Thomas Gilbert.
,, Mar.   6. Edward Dudleye.

ANNO DOMI., 1622.

1622, Apr. 7. Ann Pennye.
,, Apr. 10. Rychard, s. of Edward White.
,, Apr. 29. John Poole.
,, July 18. Elizabeth Carelesse.
,, July 22. Edward Marshe.
,, July 29. Elizabeth Probacke, a stranger.
,, Sept. 9. Symon Loe.
,, Nov. 26. The w. of John Morris.
,, Dec. 10. John Morris.
,, Dec. 29. John Pershall's wife.
,, Dec. 29. Willm. Abbats.
,, Dec. 29. The s. of John Hurleye.
162⅔, Jan. 19. Phillip White.
,, Jan. 24. The d. of Rychard Marrion.
,, Feb. 10. Frauncis, w. of George Partridg.

ANNO DOMI., 1623.

1623, Apr. 25. Willm. Jevon.
,, May   3. Ann, w. of George Woodwarde.

1623, May 19. Frauncis, wid. of John Woodward.
  ,, June 5. Ann, wid. of George Row.
  ,, June 22. The s. of Robart Ryder.
  ,, July 4. The w. of Edward Wetton.
  ,, July 25. John Pershall.
  ,, July 26. Jone Norris.
  ,, Aug. 3. Rychard Walker.
  ,, Sept. 27. John Norris.
  ,, Oct. 1. Willm. Leetham.
  ,, Nov. 2. Thomas Kirtland.
  ,, Nov. 17. Henry Rychards.
  ,, Nov. 29. Wid. Kirtland.
  ,, Dec. 4. Humphary Filkes.
162¾, Jan. 29. Marye, w. of Willm. Stanley, Esquire.
  ,, Feb. 5. Robart Jones had a child unchristened.
✓ ,, Feb. 21. John Green.
  ,, Mar. 4. Edward Pepwell.
  ,, Mar. 6. A child of Edward Norris, unchristened.

Anno Domi., 1624.

1624, June 10. Rychard Dudley had a child unchristened.
  ,, Aug. 2. Christopher Pen.
  ,, Aug. 21. Widow Stanton.
  ,, Sept. 3. Widow Syncox.
  ,, Oct. 19. John Bird.
  ,, Nov. 22. Rychard Bird.
  ,, Feb. 19. The w. of Symon Syncox.
  ,, Nov. 9. Alice, d. of Robart Jones.
  ,, Nov. 15. The s. of Willm. Forme.

Anno Domi., 1625.

1625, Apr. 24. John Jesson.
  ,, June 22. Rychard Ashley.
  ,, Aug. 15. A child of Willm. Feilding.
  ,, Sept. 5. Rychard, s. of Willm. James.
  ,, Sept. 5. A child of John Morris.
  ,, Oct. 1. Elizabeth, d. of Edward Morris.
  ,, Oct. 13. Willm. Parkes.

1625, Oct. 29. A child of Willm. Lidyate.

,, Nov. 16. Margerye, w. of Edward Beebye.

,, Nov. 20. Edward, s. of Edward Beebye.

162⅚, Jan. 11. Sybell, d. of Willm. Hollinswoorth.

,, Jan. 14. A child of Thomas Atkis.

,, Jan. 19. Willm. Partridg, of Noherhall.

,, Jan. 20. Nycholas Jesson.

,, Feb. 4. Widow Briscoe.

,, Feb. 19. Willm. Hawkes.

,, Feb. 23. Ann, w. of John Bird & her child.

ANNO DOMI., 1626.

1626, Mar. 29. A child of John Bird's.

,, Mar. 28. John Young.

,, Apr. 7. Ann, d. of John Bird.

,, Apr. 9. Willm. Hawle.

,, Apr. 21. Daniell, s. of Richard James.

,, Aug. 16. A child of Raphe Morris.

,, Aug. 28. Willm. Wright.

,, Sept. 10. A child of John Morris.

,, Sept. 13. Elizabeth Rowland *als.* Jones.

,, Sept. 22. Widow Sincox.

,, Sept. 30. Robart Foster, gent.

,, Nov. 6. A child of Willm. James.

,, Nov. 10. Elizabeth, d. of Thomas Clarke.

162⁶⁄₇, Mar. 19. Willm. Davis, a stranger.

,, Mar. 20. John, s. of Thomas Heath.

ANNO DOMI., 1627.

1627, Mar. 26. John Hodgits.

,, Mar. 31. Jone, d. of John Granger.

,, Apr. 18. Henrye Hardwick.

,, July 4. Lettice Permele.

,, July 8. Jone, w. of Humphrye Gest

,, Dec. 7. Willm., s. of John Newye.

,, Dec. 22. Elizabeth Frith.

,, Dec. 23. Margert Parkes.

162⅞, Jan.   8. Willm. Colye.
  ,, Jan.   18. Willm. Turton, thelder.
  ,, Feb.   2. Margeret Oldfeild.
  ,, Feb.   27. Margeret, w. of George Barbar.
  ,, Mar.   1. Alice, w. of John Taylor.
  ,, Mar.   9. Ann, d. of Edward Parsons *als*. Litley.
  ,, Mar.   17. Fraunces, s. of Ann Norris.

ANNO DOMI., 1628.

1628, Mar.   25. John Hides.
  ,, May   31. Willm. Wakler.
  ,, May   4. Alice, w. of Rychard Whyle.
  ,, May   14. Thomas, s. of Thomas Fidoe.
  ,, May   29. George, s. of Rychard Syncox.
  ,, June   2. John Westwood.
  ,, June   8. Jone, w. of Roger Wright.
  ,, June   9. Elizabeth, w. of Willm. Jesson.
  ,, July   6. Willm. Clare.
  ,, July 17. Edward Ashmore.
  ,, Aug.   2. Elizabeth, d. of Willm. Atkins.
  ,, Dec.   6. Phillip Ensworth.
  ,, Dec. 14. Phillip Climore.
  ,, Dec. 16. John, s. of Willm. Turton.
162⁸⁄₉, Jan.   1. Nycholas Wilye.
  ,, Jan.   7. John, s. of John Owen.
  ,, Jan.   12. Rychard, s. of Rychard Brake.
  ,, Jan.   14. John, s. of Willm. Granger.
  ,, Jan.   17. Thomas Cuntchley.
  ,, Jan.   29. Willm., s. of Thomas Bayley's.
  ,, Jan.   21. Willm. Johnson.
  ,, Mar.   3. Joseph, s. of Willm. Woodward.
  ,, Mar.   4. John, s. of Robart Jones.

ANNO DOMI., 1629.

1629, Mar.   27. John Lowe.
  ,, Mar.   31. Ann, d. of George Bird.
  ,, Apr.   4. Jone, d. of John Hawle.
  ,, Apr.   6. Elizabeth Morris.

1629.	Apr.	22.	Marye, d. of John Hawle.
,,	Apr.	28.	Thomas, s. of John Semor.
,,	May	9.	Ann, w. of Willm. Forme.
,,	May	16.	Thomas, s. of John Case.
,,	May	24.	Frauncis, s. of Willm. Forme.
,,	June	1.	Henrye, s. of Henry Newye.
,,	June	23.	Ann, d. of Willm. Forme.
,,	July	5.	Sarai, d. of Willm. Partridg.
,,	July	11.	John Gretton.
,,	July	12.	Margeret, d. of Edward Diall.
,,	July	14.	Elizabeth, d. of Willm. Marsh.
,,	Aug.	2.	Thomas Handes.
,,	Oct.	9.	Marye, w. of Rychar Wilye.
,,	Oct.	14.	Thomas Kirbye.
,,	Nov.	10.	Barbara, w. of John Coley.
,,	Nov.	14.	Thomas, s. of Rychard Tranter.
,,	Nov.	23.	Thomas, s. of Henrye Newye.
,,	Dec.	7.	Elnor, w. of Thomas Lindon.
,,	Dec.	22.	Margeret, w. of Symon Ryder.
,,	Dec.	22.	Ann Reave, wid.
,,	Dec.	25.	Edward Davis.
$16\frac{29}{36}$,	Jan.	4.	Constance Pennye.
,,	Jan.	16.	Barnabye, s. of Rychard James.
,,	Jan.	21.	Sarai, d, of John Bond.
,,	Feb.	3.	Willm. Bull.
,,	Feb.	17.	Marye, d. of Willm. Turton.
,,	Feb.	25.	Elizabeth Wiersdale.
,,	Mar.	1.	Bartholomewe More.
,,	Mar.	2.	Humphrye Jones.
,,	Mar.	2.	Rychard While.
,,	Mar.	7.	Eme Careles.
,,	Mar.	15.	George Herring.

ANNO DOMI., 1630.

1630,	May	21.	John Hawkes.
,,	May	22.	Margeret, w. of Robart Bonell.
,,	June	26.	Elizabeth, d. of George Rodes.
,,	July	17.	Elizabeth Wilson.
,,	July	17.	Rowland, s. of Rowland Bett.

1630, July 28. Jone, w. of Frauncis Briscoe.
  ,,   Aug. 4.   Thomas Woode.
  ,,   Aug. 19. Rychard, s. of Rychard Chetwin.
  ,,   Sept. 21. George, s. of Thomas Basset.   ✓
  ,,   Dec. 4.   Jane, d. of Rychard Pargiter.
  ,,   Dec. 4.   Elizabeth Colliar.
  ,,   Dec. 4.   Elizabeth, d. of Frauncis Bird.
163$\frac{0}{1}$, Jan. 29. Elizabeth, d. of Willm. James.
  ,,   Feb. 11. Jone Abbott.
  ,,   Feb. 14. Rychard Syncox.
  ,,   Mar. 7.   Thomas Browne.

Anno Domi., 1631.

1631, May   13. Jone, w. of Edward Rubotome.
  ,,   May   19. Ann, d. of Rowland Bett.
  ,,   May   21. Willm. Yardley.
  ,,   May   28. John Reevs.
  ,,   June 26. John, s. of John Rutland.
  ,,   July 14. Elnor, w. of Frauncis Syncox.
  ,,   Aug. 19. Margery Hindes.
  ,,   Aug. 19. Elizabeth Perrye, wid.
  ,,   Sept. 15. Sarai, w. of Frauncis Partridg.
  ,,   Nov. 6.   John Rychards.
  ,,   Nov. 15. Ann, d. of Willm. Lidyate.
  ,,   Dec. 7.   Frauncis, s. of Michaell Syncox.
  ,,   Dec. 28. George Barker.
  ,,   Dec. 30. John, s. of Thomas Heath.
163$\frac{1}{2}$, Jan. 3.   Ann, w. of Symon Dale.
  ,,   Jan. 20. Thomas Langam, fls. pop.
  ,,   Feb. 13. Rychard Hopkis.
  ,,   Feb. 18. Willm. Holden.
  ,,   Feb. 27. Ellen Cruchley.
  ,,   Mar. 2.   Sarai Lane.
  ,,   Mar. 7.   Mrs. Ann Shilton.
  ,,   Mar. 13. Katherine Bird.

Anno Domi., 1632.

1632, Apr. 13. Elizabeth Reeves.
  ,,   Apr. 24. Phillip, s. of Roger Osborn.

1632, May 5. Marian Jones.
  ,, May 22. Willm. Partridg.
  ,, June 3. Margert Jones.
  ,, June 3. Elnor, d. of Edward Deelye. •
  ,, June 9. Gregory Atkis.
  ,, June 22. Cassandra, w. of Thomas James *als.*
                  Stimmger.
  ,, July 5. Frauncis, s. of Willm. Reeves.
  ,, July 10. John Truelove.
  ,, July 11. John, s. of Frauncis Hodgits.
  ,, July 17. Rychard Shinger.
  ,, July 31. Jone Banner.
  ,, Sept. 15. Elizabeth, d. of John Wilye.
  ,, Sept. 25. Ann, w. of Thomas Birde.
  ,, Oct. 14. Edward, s. of Edward Diall.
  ,, Oct. 18. Symon Vale.
  ,, Oct. 21. Abraham Jesson.
  ,, Oct. 22. Marye, d. of Willm. Fildust.
  ,, Dec. 4. Iszabell, w. of Willm. Partridge.
  ,, Dec. 4. Ann, d. of John Fenton.
  ,, Dec. 25. Willm. Jesson.
163⅔, Jan. 2. The w. of John Feild.
  ,, Jan. 4. Willm., s. of Rychard Henley.
  ,, Jan. 7. John Taylor.
  ,, Jan. 21. Jone, w. of Rychard Orris.
  ,, Jan. 25. Jane, d. of Henry Frith.
  ,, Feb. 19. Margeret, w. of Edward Curtler.
  ,, Feb. 25. Thomas Tudg.
  ,, Feb. 25. Joyce Pennye.

BAPTISMS. 1632.

1632, Oct. 28. Abraham, s. of Abraham Jesson.
  ,, Oct. 28. Elizabeth, d. of Thomas Heath.
  ,, Nov. 4. Sara, d. of John Turton, Junr.
  ,, Nov. 11. Jone, d. of John Bird, Naylor.
  ,, Nov. 18. Ann, d. of John Duker.
  ,, Dec. 2. Jane, d. of Willm. Hollinsworth.
  ,, Dec. 26. Sara, d. of Willm. Syncox.

163⅔, Jan. 1. Rychard, s. of Rychard Trantor.
  ,, Jan. 6. Walter, s. of Walter Steven.
  ,, Jan. 6. John, s. of Henrye Teye.
  ,, Jan. 13. Walter, s. of Willm. Stanley.
  ,, Jan. 13. Henry, s. of Edward Sharplinge.
  ,, Jan. 13. Sara, d. of Rychard Wright.   ✓
  ,, Jan. 21. John, s. of John Fenton.
  ,, Jan. 27. John, s. of John Kirtland.
  ,, Feb. 3. George, s. of John Chetten.
  ,, Feb. 10. Humphry, s. of John Norris.
  ,, Feb. 24. Sara, d. of Willm. Bird.
  ,, Mar. 3. John, s. of Lewes Rawley.

Anno Domi., 1633.

1633, Apr. 7. Elizabeth, d. of Edward Pinkard.
  ,, Apr. 25. Sara, d. of Thomas Lytham.
  ,, June 5. Ann, d. of Henry Darby.
  ,, July 7. Alice, d. of Edward Morris.
  ,, July 10. Willm., s. of Willm. Warde.
  ,, July 14. Jane, d. of Rychard Pargiter.
  ,, Aug. 8. Rychard, s. of Willm. Blakmor.
  ,, Sept. 8. Thomas, s. of John Bird.
  ,, Sept. 15. Elizabeth, d. of Willm. James.
  ,, Sept. 15. Willm., s. of Nicholas Hodgkin.
  ,, Sept. 22. John, s. of Willm. Reeves.
  ,, Sept. 22. Thomas, s. of Thomas Basset.
  ,, Sept. 22. Ann, d. of Raphe Kendrick.
  ,, Sept. 29. Joseph, s. of Willm. Marsh.
  ,, Sept. 29. Mary, d. of Edward Dudley.
  ,, Oct. 23. Arden, s. of Thomas Freke.
  ,, Oct. 27. Jane, d. of [*omitted*] Hurley.
  ,, Nov. 3. Mary, d. of John Stamps.
  ,, Nov. 10. Willm., s. of Thomas Grove.
  ,, Nov. 17. Margery, d. of John Newhey.
  ,, Dec. 8. Joseph, s. of Rychar Bird.
  ,, Dec. 15. Thomas, s. of Edward Trantor.
  ,, Dec. 27. Frauncis, s. of Walter Stevens.
163¾, Jan. 5. George, s. of Thomas Reve.
  ,, Jan. 12. Susanna, d. of Henry Frith.

163¾,	Jan.	19.	Samuell, s. of John Frith.
,,	Jan.	26.	Ann, d. of Thomas Frith.
,,	Jan.	27.	John, s. of Frauncis Bird.
,,	Jan.	27.	Thamezen, d. of James Ferkin.
,,	Jan.	27.	Sara, d. of John Tomlinson.
,,	Jan.	27.	Willm., s. of Willm. Fildust.
,,	Jan.	27.	Sara, d. of Izac Stanton.
,,	Feb.	9.	Judeth, d. of Michell Poultney.
,,	Feb.	25.	Thomas, s. of Thomas Blackham.
,,	Feb.	25.	Margeret, d. of Raph Morris.
,,	Mar.	23.	Henry, s. of John Granger.

ANNO DOMI., 1634.

1634,	Mar.	30.	Elizabeth, d. of Willm. Rychards.
,,	Apr.	7.	John, s. of John Semer.
,,	Apr.	13.	Alice, d. of John Orice.
,,	May	1.	John, s. of Mathew Henes.
,,	May	29.	Elizabeth, d. of Frauncis Hawcks.
,,	June	1.	Katherin, d. of Willm. Rychards.
,,	June	15.	Thomas, s. of John Feild.
,,	June	29.	Sara, d. of Robart Jones.
,,	June	29.	Roberta, d. of John Warde.
,,	July	20.	Marye, d. of Edward Hodgkins.
,,	Aug.	3.	Margery, d. of Hughe Basset. ✓
,,	Aug.	3.	Sara, d. of John Parsons *als.* Littley.
,,	Aug.	31.	Frauncis, s. of Rychard Ashmore.
,,	Aug.	31.	Mary, d. of Edward Diall.
,,	Oct.	12.	John, s. of John Syncox.
,,	Oct.	12.	Mary, d. of John Wylye.
,,	Nov.	2.	John, s. of Roger Colborn.
,,	Nov.	2.	John, s. of Henry Edwards.
,,	Nov.	9.	John, s. of Willm. Stanley.
,,	Nov.	9.	Walter, s. of Frauncis Wilye.
,,	Nov.	23.	Edward, s. of Edward Dudley.
,,	Nov.	30.	Edward, s. of Thomas Atkis.
,,	Dec.	10.	Jane, d. of John Ruggley.
,,	Dec.	20.	Alice, d. of Willm. Dudley.
163⅘,	Jan.	4.	Marye, d. of John Turton.
,,	Jan.	18.	Willm., s. of Willm. Granger.

163⅘, Feb. 1. Jone, d. of Robart Brisborne.

,,   Feb. 8. Richard, s. of Rychard Reeding.

,,   Feb. 8. George, s. of Roger Chatwin.

,,   Feb. 15. Symon, s. of Willm. Birde.

,,   Feb. 15. Elizabeth, d. of John Fenton.

,,   Mar. 1. Jone, d. of John Marshe.

,,   Mar. 8. Dina, d. of George Lewis.

,,   Mar. 8. Elizabeth, d. of Thomas Morris.

,,   Mar. 8. Willm., s. of Phillip Ensworth.

,,   Mar. 15. Thomas, s. of Thomas Syncox.

,,   Mar. 19. John, s. of Isaack Stanton.

Anno Domi., 1635.

1635, Mar. 25. Mary, d. of George Bird.

,,   Apr. 12. Elenior, d. of John Chambers.

,,   Apr. 26. John, s. of Willm. Dutton.

,,   Apr. 26. Joseph, s. of Edward Sharpling.

,,   Apr. 26. Grace, d. of John Duker.

,,   Apr. 26. Elizabeth, d. of John Bird.

,,   May 6. Fils. pop., the imputed s. of Manasses Rushall.

,,   May 10. Willm., s. of Richard Partrich.

,,   May 10. Elizabeth, d. of John Hall.

,,   May 10. Mary, d. of George Sincoxe.

,,   June 28. Mary, d. of Francis Sincoxe.

,,   July 16. Sara, d. of Raphe [omitted].

,,   Aug. 2. Ann, d. of Elias Durham.

,,   Aug. 9. Thomas, s. of Nicolas Newbey.

,,   Aug. 23. Roland, s. of Roland Bett.

,,   Sept. 6. Humfrey, s. of John Case.

,,   Sept. 13. Elinor, d. of Raphe Watton.

,,   Sept. 27. Mary, d. of Willm. Richards.

,,   Sept. 29. John, s. of Richard James.

,,   Oct. 4. Joseph, s. of John Partrich.

,,   Oct. 4. Alce, d. of Thomas Heath.

,,   Oct. 6. John, s. of John Cooke.

,,   Oct. 25. Jane, d. of Nicolas Hogkins.

,,   Nov. 1. Elizabeth, d. of Willm. Fildust.

,,   Nov. 8. Ann, d. of Willm. Jones.

✓ 1635, Nov. 8. Elizabeth, d. of John Wright.
  „ Nov. 15. Francis, s. of Henry Tey.
  „ Nov. 15. Joseph, s. of Thomas Blackham.
  „ Nov. 29. Mary, d. of Francis Edwards.
  „ Nov. 29. William, s. of Richard Coxe.
✓ - „ Dec. 6. Josias, s. of John Brooke.
163⅚, Jan. 12. Josias, s. of Willm. Sincoxe.
  „ Jan. 17. Richard, s. of Richard James.
  „ Jan. 17. Thomas, s. of Willm. Hadley.
  „ Jan. 17. Elizabeth, d. of Edward Trantor.
  „ Jan. 17. Elizabeth, d. of Willm. Chetwine.
  „ Jan. 22. Henry, s. of Henry Darby.
  „ Jan. 24. Henry, s. of Henry Frythe.
  „ Jan. 31. Gregory, s. of Walter Steven.
  „ Feb. 2. John, s. of John Band.
  „ Feb. 7. George, s. of John Feild.
  „ Feb. 7. Martha, d. of Willm. Tibbats.
  „ Feb. 14. Henry, s. of Alexander Loe.
  „ Feb. 14. Sarah, d. of Raph Kenderick.
  „ Mar. 1. Elner, d. of Willm. Rowe.
  „ Mar. 4. Elizabeth, d. of Mary Bird, base born.
  „ Mar. 6. Francis, s. of Willm. Osborne.

ANNO DMI., 1636.

1636, Mar. 27. Mary, d. of Richard Trantor.
  „ Apr. 7. Francis, d. of Willm. Richards.
  „ Apr. 10. Elizabeth, d. of Willm. Sansom.
  „ Apr. 17. Raphe, s. of Richard Gretton.
  „ Apr. 17. Margret, d. of John Baker.
  „ May 15. Mary, d. of Willm. Hadley.
  „ May 22. Barbara, d. of George Stoe.
  „ May 5. Thomas, s. of Edward Dudley.
  „ May 5. Jone, d. of Thomas Manton.
  „ June 12. Mary, d. of Rich Bird.
  „ June 26. Dorothy, d. of John Semor.
  „ July 3. Thomas, s. of Francis Johnson.
  „ July 10. Mary, d. of Thomas Frith.
  „ Aug. 14. Willm., s. of Willm. Turton.
  „ Aug. 28. Unica, d. of Willm. Hollinsworth.

1636, Aug.	28.	John, s. of Francis Hoggets.
,, Sept.	4.	Thomas, s. of John Noris.
,, Sept.	13.	Elizabeth, d. of John Sincoxe.
,, Oct.	7.	John, s. of Robart Jones.
,, Oct.	25.	Ann, d. of George Payne.
,, Nov.	13.	Willm., s. of Thomas Sewell.
,, Nov.	13.	Thomas, s. of Francis Bird.

THOMAS JONSON, Minister.

,, Nov.	20.	Henrey, s. of Henrey Was.
,, Nov.	20.	Sarah, d. of John Round.
,, Nov.	27.	Thomas, s. of Thomas Jesson.
,, Dec.	18.	Jonathan, s. of John Frith.
163$\frac{6}{7}$, Jan.	6.	Jone, d. of Alexander Woodward.
,, Jan.	8.	Jane, d. of Thomas Litham.
,, Jan.	22.	George, s. of Mathew Lewes.
,, Jan.	22.	Sarah, d. of Willm. Sterey.
,, Jan.	29.	Thomas, s. of Willm. Partrich.
,, Jan.	29.	George, s. of John Kirtland.
,, Feb.	5.	Alexander, s. of Richard Partrich.
,, Feb.	5.	Judeth, d. of James Felkin.
,, Feb.	5.	Sara, d. of Richard Coxe.
,, Feb.	12.	John, s. of John Duker.
,, Feb.	12.	Raph, s. of John Marsh.
,, Feb.	16.	Hanna, d. of Mr. Thomas Johnson.
,, Feb.	4.	Luce, d. of Willm. Stanley.

THOMAS GROVE,
JOHN BIRD, } Economis.

1637.

1637, Apr.	30.	Sara, d. of Willm. James.
,, May	7.	Willm., s. of John Staunts.
,, May	7.	Joseph, s. of Roger Coleburne.
,, May	21.	Alice, d. of Walter & Elizabeth Steeven.
,, May	23.	Geffery, s. of John & Elinor Cooke.
,, May	23.	Susanna, d. of George & Margeret Robbins.
,, June	30.	Sarah, d. of Hugh & Mary Bassett.
,, July	2.	Walter, s. of John & Elizabeth Wyley.

1637, July	2.	Henry, s. of Henry & Alice Frith.	
,, July	6.	Flo. pop., the bast. s. of Ann Rowbotham.	
,, July	23.	Samuel, s. of Willm. Partridge.	
,, July	30.	Elizabeth, d. of Edward & Anne Dudley.	
,, Aug.	6.	John, s. of John & Mary Bird.	
,, Aug.	6.	Joseph, s. of Lewis & Alice Raweley.	
,, Aug.	6.	Robert, s. of Willm. & Anne Grice.	
,, Sept.	10.	Gregory, s. of Willm. & Margeret Bird.	
,, Sept.	10.	John, s. of Michael & Jane Pary.	
,, Sept.	10.	Willm., s. of Thomas & Jane Syncox.	
,, Sept.	24.	Abigaill, d. of Francis & Alice Syncox.	
,, Oct.	8.	Willm., s. of John & Elizabeth Horton.	
,, Oct.	8.	Willm., s. of Roland & Anne Bock.	
,, Oct.	15.	Thomas, s. of Thomas Hurley.	
,, Oct.	15.	John, s. of John & Alice Baker.	
,, Oct.	31.	Henry, s. of Thomas Cashmore.	
,, Nov.	19.	Hannah, d. of Thomas & Mary Reinolds.	
,, Dec.	3.	Dorothy, d. of Richard & Margery James.	
,, Dec.	10.	Robert, s. of John & Frances Granger.	
,, Dec.	10.	Anna, d. of Edward & Mary Dudley.	
,, Dec.	17.	Joseph, s. of Thomas & Cicely Morris.	
163⅞, Jan.	7.	Mary, d. of Henry & Dorothy Tey.	
,, Jan.	14.	Joan, d. of Francis & Sara Wiley.	
,, Jan.	14.	Sara, d. of Richard Ashmore.	
,, Jan.	28.	Willm., s. of Raphe & Judeth Malton.	
,, Feb.	4.	Samuel, s. of Richard & Ann Reading.	
,, Feb.	4.	Henry, s. of Edward & Anne Wilcox.	
,, Feb.	11.	John, s. of Thomas & Elizabeth Underhill.	
,, Feb.	18.	Sara, d. of Thomas Heale.	
,, Feb.	18.	Agnes, d. of Willm. Shenton.	
,, Feb.	25.	Joan, d. of John Oris.	
,, Feb.	25.	Joseph, s. of Thomas idkman.	
,, Mar.	4.	Francis, s. of Thomas Dutton.	
,, Mar.	4.	Thomas, s. of George Aplewis.	
,, Mar.	18.	William, s. of John & Joan Fenton.	
,, Mar.	18.	Jane, d. of Henry & Catherine Wasse.	
,, Mar.	22.	William, s. of Michaell Poulton.	

THOMAS JESSON, }
WILLIAM STERRY, } Economis.

Anno Domi., 1638.

1638,	May	10.	Thomas, s. of John & Dorothy Seamore.
,,	May	14.	Thomas, s. of John & Dorothy Seamer.
,,	June	3.	Ales, d. of William & Anne Fildust.
,,	June	28.	Thomas, s. of Thomas & Elizabeth Willoughby.
,,	July	6.	Edward, s. of Edward & Ann Deeley.
,,	July	29.	Joyce, d. of Thomas & Elizabeth Wiersdale.
,,	Aug.	26.	Thomas, s. of William & Ann Granger.
,,	Aug.	26.	Sarah, d. of William & Mary Rowe.
,,	Aug.	26.	Elizabeth, d. of Willm. & Elizabeth Richards.
,,	Sept.	2.	Joseph, s. of John & Judeth Reinolds.
,,	Sept.	2.	Thomas, s. of John & Katherine Wright.
,,	Sept.	9.	William, s. of George & Amy Stowe.
,,	Sept.	30.	George, s. of William & Mary Partridge.
,,	Sept.	30.	John, s. of Edward & Mary Hodgkins.
,,	Oct.	14.	Margret, d. of George & Alce Rowe.
,,	Oct.	21.	Jone, d. of Robert & Anne Marsh.
,,	Nov.	4.	Anne, d. of Thomas & Mary Frith.
,,	Nov.	11.	William, s. of Hughe & Elizabeth Niccolls.
,,	Nov.	18.	Robert, s. of Thomas & Elonar Blackham.
,,	Nov.	20.	Henry, s. of Thomas & Jane Bassage.
,,	Dec.	2.	George, s. of Thomas & Mary Jesson.
,,	Dec.	2.	Hateley, s. of Water & Ellonar Dale.
,,	Dec.	9.	William, s. of William & Isabell Winser.
,,	Dec.	26.	Rebecca, d. of William & Frances Richards.
,,	Dec.	29.	John, s. of John Byrd.
163$\frac{8}{9}$,	Feb.	3.	Susanna, d. of Nicholas & Jane Hodgins.
,,	Mar.	3.	Willm., s. of Willm. & Joyce Hadley.
,,	Mar.	3.	Abigall, d. of John & Elizabeth Morris.
,,	Mar.	10.	Hugh, s. of George Basset.
,,	Mar.	24.	William, s. of William & Mary Stanley.
,,	Mar.	12.	Edward, s. of John & Abigail Sincox.

Anno Dmi., 1639.

1639,	Mar.	31.	Sarah, d. of Edward & Anne Traunter.
,,	Apr.	7.	Margaret, d. of Water & Elizabeth Stephene.
,,	Apr.	15.	Joseph, s. of John & Anne Coleman.
,,	Apr.	21.	Elizabeth, d. of William & Ellnor Wall.

1639, May   1.　Ellonar, d. of John & Ellonar Brooks.
　,,　June   3.　Mary, d. of Edward & Anne Dudley.
　,,　June 16.　Sara, d. of William & John Partrich.
　,,　July 21.　Edward, s. of Edward & Jane Peppall.
　,,　July 21.　Judeth, d. of Edward & Mary Dudley.
　,,　Aug.   4.　Jone, d. of William & Magdalen Allen.
　,,　Aug. 18.　Mary, d. of Henry & Jone Edwards.
　,,　Sept. 1.　John, s. of William & Ellonar Partrich.
　,,　Sept. 1.　John, s. of Edward & Anne Mordick.
　,,　Sept. 15.　Christopher, s. of Henry Darby.
　,,　Sept. 22.　Alice, d. of Edmund & Mary Wiley.
　,,　Sept. 29.　John, s. of John & Elizabeth Edwards.
　,,　Sept. 29.　Elizabeth, d. of George & Margaret Robbins.
　,,　Nov. 10.　William, s. of William Smith.
　,,　Nov. 10.　Paul, s. of Alexander & Sarah Lowe.
　,,　Nov. 10.　Mary, d. of Francis & Anne Dekin.
　,,　Dec.   8.　Joseph, s. of Hughe & Mary Bassage.
　,,　Dec. 20.　Elizabeth, d. of John Marsh.
16$\frac{39}{40}$, Jan. 26.　John, s. of Francis & Elizabeth Powton.
　,,　Jan. 26.　Anne, d. of Thomas & Jane Syncox.
　,,　Feb.   2.　Job, s. of Roger & Mary Coleburn.
　,,　Feb.   2.　Anne, d. of Richard & Mary Partrich.
　,,　Feb. 16.　William, s. of William & Isabell Whyte.
　,,　Feb. 16.　Elizabeth, d. of John & Mary Byrd.
　,,　Mar.   1.　George, s. of Richard & Lucy Hanson.
　,,　Mar.   1.　Sarah, d. of John & Alice Duker.
　,,　Mar.   8.　Mary, d. of Raphe & Judeth Wotton.

Anno Dmi., 1640.

1640, Mar. 25.　Mary, d. of William & Isabell Hadley.
　,,　Apr.   1.　Edward, s. of John & Elizabeth Stonely.
　,,　Apr. 25.　Jane, d. of William & Elizabeth Shelfield.
　,,　May   3.　Hanna, d. of Izack & Dorothy Stanton.
　,,　May 10.　Elizabeth, d. of John & Elizabeth Wyley.
　,,　May 24.　Mary, d. of William & Margaret Gilbert.
　,,　May 24.　Michaell, s. of George & Joyce Sincox.
　,,　June 24.　Katherine, d. of Susanna Smith, unlawfully
　　　　　　　begotten.
　,,　July   2.　John, s. of William & Frances Richards.

1640, July	5.	Francis, s. of Francis Thornton.
,, July	5.	Robert, s. of John & Ellonar Croke.
,, July	12.	William, s. of Thomas & Mary Jesson.
,, July	12.	Joseph, s. of Francis & Sarah Wyley.
,, Aug.	2.	Anne, d. of William & Mary Partrich.
,, Aug.	2.	Anne, d. of Richard & Elizabeth Cox.
,, Aug.	2.	John, s. of John & Joyce Parsons.
,, Aug.	9.	Josias, s. of Lewis & Alice Rawley.
,, Aug.	9.	Ellonar, d. of Thomas & Jone Edwards.
,, Aug.	16.	Mary, d. of Richard & Ellonar Stringer.
,, Aug.	23.	Mary, d. of Willm. & Ann Turton.
,, Aug.	30.	William, s. of William & Anne Grice.
,, Aug.	30.	Mary, d. of John & Dorothy Seamore.
,, Aug.	19.	Moses, s. of Richard & Margery James.
,, Sept.	27.	Edward, s. of John & Jone Fenton.
,, Sept.	27.	Elizabeth, d. of Thomas & Elizabeth Wyersdale.
,, Oct.	4.	Alice, d. of John & Alice Baker.
,, Oct.	18.	George, s. of George & Mary Basset.
,, Nov.	8.	Thomas, s. of Thomas & Mary Gilbert.
,, Nov.	8.	Eunice, d. of Thomas & Ellonar Blackham.
,, Nov.	15.	Thomas, s. of John & Elizabeth Horton.
,, Nov.	15.	Elizabeth, d. of William & Judeth Turton.
,, Nov.	22.	Thomas, s. of Henry & Katherine Wasse.
,, Nov.	22.	William, s. of William & Ellonar Wall.
164$\frac{0}{1}$, Jan.	1.	Raph, s. of John & Minerva Marsh.
,, Jan.	8.	Willm., s. of Willm. & Mari Rowe.
,, Jan.	10.	Thomas, s. of Edward & Ann Dudley.
,, Jan.	10.	John, s. of Richard & Mary Tranter
,, Jan.	10.	Francis, s. of Francis & An Dekin.
,, Jan.	10.	Elizabeth, d. of Nicholas & Jane Hogkins.
,, Mar.	7.	Anne, d. of Edward & Anne Traunter.
,, Mar.	7.	Elizabeth, d. of Edward & Jane Peppall.
,, Feb.	28.	Elizabeth, d. of Thomas & Margaret Dutton.
,, Mar.	21.	Rowland, s. of Rowland & Anne Bett.

Ano Dmi., 1641.

| 1641, Feb. | 28. | Mary, d. of Robert & Anne Marsh. |
| ,, Apr. | 4. | Thomas, s. of John & Abigaile Sincox. |

1641, Apr.   4. Ellonar, d. of Edward Wilcox.
,, Apr. 18. Mary, d. of William & Jone Partrich.
,, Apr. 26. Henry, s. of Henry & Dorothy Eade.
,, Apr. 27. Elizabeth, d. of Edward & Mary Fenton.
,, Apr. 27. Sarah, d. of William & Joyce Hadley.
,, May 16. John, s. of John & Judith Reinolds.
,, May 16. Elizabeth, d. of Alexander & Margaret Woodward.
,, May 16. Elizabeth, d. of Francis & Frances Edwards.
,, May 30. George, s. of John & Winifrede Bertinsson.
,, July   4. William, s. of Francis & Elizabeth Poultney.
,, July   5. Hugh, s. of Hugh & Elizabeth Morris.
,, May 30. Mary, d. of John & Anne Orris.
,, Dec.   5. Abigaile, d. of Thomas & Mary Gilbert.
✓ ,, Oct. 20. Mary, d. of John & Ellonar Brooks.
,, Dec. 12. Edward, s. of Isaac & Dorothy Stanton.
,, Sept. 26. Sarah, d. of Richard Bird.
164½, Jan.   2. Sarah, d. of John & Mary Bird.
,, Jan. 16. John, s. of Michaell Sincox.
,, Jan. 23. Sarah, d. of William Winser.
,, Feb.   6. Rebecca, d. of Francis Sincox.
,, Feb. 13. Alice, d. of Henry & Mary Averill.

ANNO DMI., 1642.

1642, May   8. Francis, s. of William & Mary Partrich.
,, May 15. Jane, d. of Thomas & Jane Bassage.
,, June   5. Martha, d. of Robert & Susanna Blaksley.
,, July   3. Margaret, d. of William & Katherine Bott.
,, Aug. 24. William, s. of George & Mary Robsart.
,, Aug. 28. John, s. of Thomas & Margaret Jesson.
,, Sept. 11. William, s. of Edward & Mary Badley.
,, Sept. 25. Sarah, d. of Thomas & Ellonar Blackams.
,, Oct. 30. John, s. of Raphe & Katherine Stanley.
,, Oct. 30. Elizabeth, d. of Robert & Elizabeth Gretton.
,, Nov. 20. Elizabeth, d. of John & Dorothy Seamore.
,, Nov. 28. Elizabeth, d. of Richard & Grace Jones.
,, Nov. 28. Elizabeth, d. of William & Elizabeth Shelfield.
,, Nov. 28. Sara, d. of John & Jone Fenton.

1642, Dec.	11.	Mary, d. of Edward & Anne Trantor.
,, Dec.	13.	Joan, d. of William & Frances Richards.
,, Dec.	18.	Mary, d. of Edward & Frances Curtler.
,, Dec.	25.	William, s. of William Blakemore.
,, Dec.	26.	Jone, d. of John & Elizabeth Wyley.
,, Dec.	26.	Anne, d. of John & Alice Baker.
,, Dec.	27.	Margery, d. of Francis & Sara Wyley.
164⅔, Jan.	8.	Thomas, s. of Francis & Isabell Johnson.
,, Jan.	15.	Thomas, s. of Thomas & Alver Reede.
,, Jan.	22.	Alice, d. of Thomas & Katherine Salt.
,, Jan.	29.	William, s. of William Penney.
,, Jan.	29.	Jone, d. of Nicholas Ockley.
,, Feb.	2.	Francis, s. of Francis & Elizabeth Poultney.
,, Feb.	5.	William, s. of Thomas & Jone Edwards.
,, Feb.	12.	Ellonar, d. of William & Ellonar Wall.
,, Feb.	19.	John, s. of John & Dorothy Bissell.
,, Feb.	19.	John, s. of Willm. & Jone Partrich.
,, Mar.	5.	Katheren, d. of Richard & Ellinor James.
,, Mar.	5.	John, s. of William Wotton, of Walsall.
,, Mar.	12.	John, s. of William & Isabell Winsor.
,, Mar.	12.	Rebeca, d. of An Gowes.
,, Mar.	19.	Mary, d. of Francis Thornton.
1643, Apr.	30.	Elizabeth, d. of Nicolas & Elizabeth Drewry.
,, May	7.	Francis, s. of Francis & Elizabeth Sincoxe.
,, May	21.	Elizabeth, d. of John & Elizabeth Thornton.
,, May	23.	Sarah, d. of John & Elinor Ward.
,, June	4.	Mary, d. of Roger Colborne.
,, June	4.	Mary, d. of Richard Trantor.
,, June	18.	Ann, d. of Edward Dudley.
,, July	16.	George, s. of George Rowe.
,, July	16.	Margaret, d. of George Stoe.
,, July	16.	Elizabeth, d. of Thomas Atkins.

EDWARD [LANE].

,, Aug.	6.	Hanna, d. of George Robsart.
,, Aug.	6.	Martha, d. of Willm. Stanley.
,, Aug.	20.	Robart, s. of Robart Merihurst.
,, Aug.	20.	Sarah, d. of Willm. Partrich, Buckelmaker.
,, Aug.	24.	Alce, d. of Hendry Sawbey.
,, Aug.	27.	Jane, d. of John Watson, of Wedensbury.

1643, Sept. 17. Mary, d. of Lewes Rawley.

,,   Sept. 24. Hendry, s. of Hendry Edwards.

,,   Sept. 24. Nicolas, s. of Nicolas Hodgkins.

,,   Oct.   1. Hendry, s. of Thomas Fryth.

,,   Oct.   1. John, s. of John Renolds.

,,   Oct.   8. Elizabeth, d. of Robart Turner.

,,   Nov. 12. Elizabeth, d. of Hendry Ley.

,,   Nov. 19. Ann, d. of Willm. Reve.

,,   Nov. 19. Ann, d. of Morris Baker.

,,   Dec.   3. Jone, d. of Francis Edwards.

,,   Dec. 10. Hendry, s. of Hugh Basset.   ✓

,,   Dec. 10. John, s. of Water Wiley.

,,   Dec. 17. Elizabeth, d. of Edward Dudley.

,,   Dec. 24. John, s. of Edward Flecher.

,,   Dec. 24. Elizabeth, d. of Robart Marsh.

,,   Dec. 24. John, s. of Edward Peppall.

164¾, Jan.   6. Elizabeth, d. of John Cam.

,,   Feb. 25. Francis & Thomas Wiersdale.

,,   Mar. 17. George, s. of Thomas Basset.   ✓

,,   Mar. 24. Thomas, s. of Willm. Fildust.

,,   Mar. 24. John, s. of Richard Carles.

,,   Mar. 24. Willm., s. of Willm. Taylor.

1644, Mar. 25. Margaret, d. of William Turner.

,,   Mar. 31. Thomas, s. of Thomas Rooker.

,,   Apr. 21. John, s. of William Cox.

,,   Apr. 22. Hanna, d. of John Horton.

,,   Apr. 22. Elizabeth, d. of Hendry Avrill.

,,   June 30. Hanna, d. of Willm. Osborne.

,,   July   7. Francis, s. of Thomas Sincox.

,,   July   7. John, s. of John Baker.

,,   July 21. Edward, s. of Richard Partrich.

,,   July 21. An, d. of William Wiley.

,,   July 21. Elizabeth, d. of Thomas Sincox.

,,   July 21. Mary, d. of John Bird.

,,   July 21. Thomas, s. of the Wid. Basset.   ✓

,,   Aug. 11. Edward, s. of Thomas Jesson.

,,   Aug. 18. Hendry, s. of Willm. Partrich.

,,   Aug. 18. Edward, s. of Roland Bets.

,,   Aug. 25. Willm., s. of John Gomer.

1644, Aug. 25.   Robart, s. of Hendry Bate.
  ,,   Sept. 22.   Ann, d. of John Brooks.   ✓   ℮ℐ
  ,,   Sept. 22.   Abigall, d. of John Walker.
  ,,   Sept. 29.   John, s. of Edward Cùrtler.
  ,,   Sept. 29.   Winifred, d. of John Beedonson.
  ,,   Oct.   6.   Mary, d. of Edward Fenton.
  ,,   Oct. 27.   Elizabeth, d. of Robart Turner.
  ,,   Nov.   3.   Alexander, s. of Alexander Jarvis.
  ,,   Nov. 24.   Hugh, s. of Hughe Harper.
  ,,   Nov. 24.   Mary, d. of Richard James.
  ,,   Dec.   1.   Jane, d. of Raphe Stanley.
  ,,   Dec. 15.   Thomas, s. of Hugh Merihurst.
  ,,   Dec. 21.   Jane, d. of Jane Jones.
  ,,   Dec. 22.   Michaell, s. of Michaell Sincoxe.
  ,,   Dec. 22.   John, s. of Randall Smalwood.
  ,,   Dec. 26.   Elizabeth, d. of William Grise.
  ,,   Dec. 29.   John, s. of Edmond Wiley.
  ,,   Dec. 29.   John, s. of Gregory Avans.
  ,,   Dec. 29.   Elliner, d. of Water Stevens.
1644⅘, Jan. 12.   William, s. of William Bird.
  ,,   Jan. 12.   Samuwell, s. of Thomas Moris.
  ,,   Jan. 19.   Hendry, s. of William Wall.
  ,,   Jan. 19.   Mary, d. of Francis Partrich.
  ,,   Jan. 19.   Unica, d. of Edward Dudley.
  ,,   Jan. 26.   Joseph, s. of Josephe Jarvis.
  ,,   Feb.   9.   Mary, d. of Willm. Osabee, of Olbery.
  ,,   Feb. 16.   Roberta, d. of Edward Traunter.
  ,,   Feb. 23.   Edward, s. of William Blakemore.
  ,,   Feb. 23.   William, s. of William Shelfeild.
       [*Added in a later hand and red ink*] 1648. Mary, d.
                    of William Shelfeld.
  ,,   Mar.   2.   Rebeka & Hana, ds. of William Partrich.
  ,,   Mar.   9.   John, s. of John Thornton.
  ,,   Mar.   9.   Ann, d. of Nicolas Drewry.
  ,,   Mar. 23.   William, s. of William While.
1645, Mar. 30.   Thomas, s. of John Eade.
  ,,   Mar. 30.   John, s. of John Cox.
  ,,   Mar. 30.   Ann, d. of Hendry Wasse.
  ,,   Apr. 27.   Mary, d. of Mr. Edward Lane, Minister.

1645, May	.	Thomas, s. of Thomas Chasmore.
,,	June	.	Thomas, s. of George Jesson.
,,	June	4	Raphe, s. of Francis Wiley.
,,	June	₄:	Edward, s. of Edward Dudley.
,,	June	8.	Ann, d. of John Wiley.
,,	June	15.	Jone, d. of John Cole.
,,	June	22.	Thomas, s. of Willm. White.
,,	June	22.	Elizabeth, d. of Francis Liddiat.
,,	June	6 (*sic ? July*).	Robart, s. of John Fenton.
,,	Aug.	3.	Ann, d. of James Ewans.
,,	Aug.	3.	Francis, d. of Willm. Lidiate.
,,	Aug.	3.	Elizabeth, d. of Richard James.
,,	Aug.	3.	Hana & Jone, ds. of John Atkins.
,,	Aug.	5.	John, s. of John Calme.
,,	Aug.	10.	John, s. of John Baker.
,,	Aug.	12.	Elizabeth, d. of John Ward.
,,	Aug.	17.	Ann, d. of Thomas Stanton.
,,	Aug.	31.	Jone, d. of John Edwards.
,,	Sept.	14.	Richard, s. of Richard Jones.
,,	Sept.	28.	Edward, s. of Edward Cole.
,,	Sept.	28.	Margret, d. of Hendry Medowes.
,,	Sept.	28.	Dorothy, d. of Hendry Edwards.
,,	Oct.	12.	John, s. of William Osborne.
,,	Oct.	12.	Ann, d. of Nickholas Okeley.
,,	Oct.	19.	Willm., s. of Francis Thornton.
,,	Nov.	23.	Willm., s. of Gregory Avans.
,,	Dec.	20.	Thomas [*erased*], s. of Thomas Hadley.
,,	Dec.	14.	John, s. of Thomas Stanley.
,,	Dec.	14.	John, s. of Francis Partrich, of Warly
,,	Dec.	14.	Ann, d. of Willm. Partrich.
,,	Dec.	21.	Richard, s. of Hugh Harper.
,,	Dec.	21.	Joyce, d. of Thomas Frith.
,,	Dec.	28.	Sara & Jone, ds. of George Basset. ✔
,,	Dec.	28.	James, s. of Willm. Turner.
164⅚, Jan.	18.	Willm., s. of William Richards.
,,	Jan.	25.	Hanna, d. of Samuel Higgens.
,,	Feb.	1.	Joseph, s. of Michael Sincoxe.
,,	Feb.	1.	Thomas, s. of Thomas Tuncks.
,,	Feb.	1.	Ann, d. of Robart Merihurst.

164⅚, Feb. 1. Frances, d. of Water Fenton.

,, Feb. 15. Thomas, s. of Thomas Gilbart.

,, Feb. 22. Elizabeth, d. of Hendry Darby.

,, Mar. 8. Richard, s. of Richard Carles.

,, Mar. 8. Frances, d. of George Sincox.

,, Mar. 18. Elizabeth, d. of William Wiley.

1646.

1646, Mar. 31. Richard, s. of Robart Flint.

,, Apr. 19. John, s. of Izack Hall.

,, Apr. 26. Willm. & Elinor, s. & d. of John Renolds.

,, May 9. Margret, d. of Edward Dudley.

,, May 16. Goodeth, d. of John Feild.

,, May 18. John, s. of Francis Sincoxe.

,, May 18. Jerome, s. of Willm. Chatwin.

,, May 29. John, s. of Mr. Morton.

,, May 29. John, s. of Nicolas Hogkins.

,, June 10. Elizabeth, d. of John Best.

,, June 17. Richard & Sara, s. & d. of Willm. Winsor.

,, June 24. Jane, d. of Thomas Blackham.

,, July 19. Obediah, s. of Lewes Rawley.

,, July 19. Jone, d. of John Duger.

Per me ED. LANE.

,, Sept. 13. Joseph, s. of Thomas Jesson.

,, Sept. 13. Willm., s. of John Atkins.

,, Nov. 29. Elizabeth, d. of Thomas Boot.

,, Nov. 30. Willm., s. of Willm. Partrich.

,, Nov. 30. Raphe, s. of Robart Morsh.

,, Dec. 19. Mary, d. of Willm. Taylor.

,, Dec. 20. Thomas, s. of Thomas Hadley.

,, Dec. 20. Sara, d. of Edward Sincox.

,, Dec. 27. John, s. of John Tomson.

164⁶₇, Jan. 17. Thomas, s. of Willm. Cox.

,, Jan. 17. Alce, d. of John Bird.

,, Feb. 17. Thomas, s. of Willm. Wall.

,, Feb. 28. Edeth, d. of Willm. Wiley.

,, Mar. 3. Thomas, s. of Thomas Sincoxe.

,, Mar. 3. Richard, s. of Thomas Stanton, at Coventrey.

1647.

1647, Apr. 17. Elizabeth, d. of John Baker, at Wedbery.
,, Apr. 17. Ann, d. of Willm. Hadley, at Wednesbury.
,, May 25. Sara, d. of Edward Dudley.
,, June 7. John, s. of George Marsh.
,, July 3. John, s. of Willm. Wiley.
,, Sept. 7. Thomas, s. of Thomas Morris.
,, Oct. 11. Willm., s. of Hendry Free.
,, Oct. 11. Edward, s. of Henry Wasse.
,, Oct. 31. John, s. of John Hurse.
,, Oct. 31. John, s. of Thomas Wiersdale.
,, Oct. 31. Hester, d. of Willm. Partrich.
,, Oct. 31. Elizabeth, d. of John Lester.
,, Nov. 3. Ann, d. of Roger Biddell.
,, Dec. 28. John, s. of John Ward.
164⅞, Jan. 30. Sara, d. of Richard Storey.
,, Feb. 10. Elizabeth, d. of Henry Cookes.
,, Feb. 10. Roger, s. of John Bedonson.

1648.

1648, June 13. Jone, d. of Richard James.
,, June 27. Sara, d. of John Sincox.
,, June 27. Ann, d. of John Baker.
    The first that was baptized by Richard Hilton was—
,, July 30. William, s. of Thomas Tuncks.
,, Aug. 13. John, s. of John Deley.
,, Aug. 20. George, s. of John Fenton.
,, Sept. 3. Robart, s. of John Semer.
,, Sept. 30. Margret, d. of John Cox.
,, Oct. 7. Dorothy, d. of Willm. Osborne.
,, Oct. 8. John, s. of John Perks.
,, Oct. 8. Mary, d. of Thomas Hadley.
,, Nov. 5. Richard, s. of Roland Bett.
,, Nov. 19. John, s. of Robart Merihurst.
,, Nov. 19. Mary, d. of Richard Partrich.
,, Nov. 26. Elen, d. of Edward Dixson.
,, Dec. 3. John, s. of John Calme.
,, Dec. 10. Edward, s. of Edward Hill.

1648, Dec. 18.   Ann, d. of Thomas Read.

„   Dec. 31.   George, s. of Willm. Partrich.

164⁸⁄₉, Jan. 7.   John, s. of John Gadd.

„   Jan. 14.   Edward, s. of Willm. Tarper.

„   Jan. 21.   Samuell, s. of Samuell Hopkins.

„   Jan. 21.   John, s. of John Hurst.

„   Feb. 11.   Thomas, s. of Willm. Winser.

„   Feb. 11.   Hendry, s. of Robart Stanley.

„   Feb. 18.   Thomas, s. of Izack Fildust.

„   Feb. 18.   Mary, d. of Thomas Dutton.

„   Feb. 22.   Ann, d. of Willm. Richards.

„   Feb. 25.   Thomas, s. of Thomas Whitbye.

„   Mar. 4.   Elizabeth, d. of Richard Carlis.

„   Mar. 18.   Elnor, d. of Edward Dudley.

„   Mar. 18.   Jone, d. of Willm. Lidiat.

1649.

1649, Mar. 25.   Mary, d. of Robart Turner.

„   Apr. 1.   John, s. of Nicholas Ockley.

„   Apr. 8.   John, s. of Walter Steven.

„   Apr. 15.   Sara, d. of John Cole.

„   May 11.   Mary, d. of Willm. Jesson.

„   July 1.   Joseph, s. of Hendry Edwards.

„   Oct. 12.   Elinor, d. of Thomas Cashmore.

„   Nov. 20.   Mary, d. of Richard Stery.

„   Dec. 7.   Izacke, s. of Izacke Hall.

„   Nov. 26.   John, s. of Robart Turner.

„   Dec. 16.   Dorothy, d. of John Foster.

164⁴⁹₅₀, Jan. 6.   Margret, d. of George Biram.

„   Feb. 27.   Richard, s. of Nicholas Hogkins.

„   Feb. 20.   Thomas, s. of Richard Aston.

„   Feb. 20.   Mary, d. of Willm. Wiley.

„   Feb. 24.   Edward, s. of Willm. White.

„   Feb. 27.   Ann, d. of John Stokes.

„   Mar. 5.   Ann, d. of Thomas Sincox.

„   Mar. 17.   Joseph, s. of John Ward.

„   Mar. 24.   Jane, d. of Willm. Wiley.

„   Mar. 24.   Ann, d. of Willm. Taylor.

„   Mar. 24.   John, s. of Thomas Morris.

1650.

1650, Mar. 31.	Willm., s. of Willm. Osborne.
,, Apr. 7.	Willm., s. of Willm. Partrich.
,, Apr. 21.	John, s. of Willm. Peney.
,, Apr. 21.	Thomas, s. of Thomas Ashmore.
,, May 12.	Hanna, d. of Michaell Sincox.
,, June 23.	Izacke, s. of John Baker.
,, June 23.	Mary, d. of Samuell Higins.
,, Aug. 25.	Elizabeth, d. of Edward Dudley.
,, Oct. 6.	Mary, d. of Richard Jesson.
,, Oct. 6.	Ann, d. of John Calme.
,, Oct. 13.	Martha, d. of Roger Colborne.
,, Oct. 20.	Willm., s. of Edward Dudley, the elder.
,, Oct. 20.	Judeth, d. of John Ward, Junr.
,, Nov. 3.	Thomas, s. of John Tomson.
,, Nov. 17.	Hendry, s. of Hendry Darby.
,, Nov. 17.	Mary, d. of Francis Thornton.
,, Nov. 24.	John, s. of Willm. Wall.
,, Nov. 24.	John, s. of John Hall.
,, Dec. 2.	Elias, s. of John Lester.
,, Dec. 7.	Ann, d. of Willm. Cox.
,, Dec. 12.	Elizabeth, d. of Willm. Turton.
,, Dec. 22.	Willm., s. of Thomas Fryth.
,, Dec. 22.	Margret, d. of Isacke Fildust.
165⁰⁄₁, Jan. 5.	Thomas, s. of John Henton.
,, Jan. 12.	Hester, d. of Hendry Meadowes.
,, Jan. 15.	Elizabeth, d. of Thomas Stanley.
,, Feb. 9.	Joseph, s. of Hendry Averell.
,, Feb. 9.	Joseph, s. of Gregory
,, Feb. 9.	Mary, d. of John Barker.
,, Feb. 24.	Moses Bird.

BURIALS. 1633.

1633, Mar. 29.	Thomas, s. of Willm. Jones.
,, Apr. 2.	Morris Jones was [*sic.* Ap. ?] Jones.
,, Apr. 19.	Frauncis Syncox.
,, Apr. 30.	Iszabell Hodgins.
,, [May] 4.	Thomas Orme.

1633, June	2.	Mary Collyar.
,, June	8.	Frauncis Clare.
,, June	12.	George Woodward.
,, June	21.	Ann Saunders, wid.
,, June	28.	Ann Mosse.
,, Aug.	10.	Thomas Masse.
,, Oct.	6.	Joseph, s. of Willm. Marsh.
,, Oct.	13.	John, s. of Thomas Clarke.
,, Oct.	25.	Widow Keeling.
,, Nov.	27.	Roger Frith.
,, Nov.	24.	Thomas, s. of Willm. Turton.
163¾, Mar.	2.	Sara, d. of Izack Stanton.
,, Mar.	10.	Edward Reinolds.
,, Mar.	21.	Mawde Parks.

ANNO DOMI., 1634.

1634, Mar.	30.	Ann Shropsheir *als.* Baker.
,, Apr.	25.	Edward Rowbotham.
,, May	21.	Frauncis, w. of John Chetwin.
,, June	22.	Mary, d. of Willm. Lidyat.
,, June	29.	John, s. of John Case.
,, July	6.	Henry, s. of Edward Sharplin.
,, July	9.	David Owen.
,, Aug.	4.	Elizabeth, d. of Wid. Tudge.
,, Aug.	19.	Margeret, d. of Raph Morris.
,, Nov.	10.	Alice, d. of Thomas Blackham.
,, Nov.	19.	Willm., s. of Willm. Feildust.
,, Dec.	13.	Thomas Deely.
,, Dec.	25.	Frauncis Greene.
,, Dec.	26.	Marye, w. of Willm. James *al.* Stringer.
,, Dec.	31.	Frauncis, s. of Frauncis Ellis, peregrinus.
163⁴⁄₅, Jan.	9.	John, s. of Thomas Dutton.
,, Jan.	27.	Alice, d. of Willm. Hadley.
,, Jan.	29.	Willm. Hokben.
,, Jan.	29.	John, s. of Gregorye Woodward.

ANNO DOMI., 1635.

1635, Apr.	15.	John Deely.
,, Apr.	15.	Jane Okill.

1635, Apr. 19. John Dolphin.
„   Apr. 25. Simon Newhey.
„   May 19. Ann, w. of Adam Turton.
„   June 5. Willm. Sincoxe.
„   July 1. Samuel Johnson.
„   July 10. Ann Herring, wid.
„   July 18. Thomas Stoney.
„   Aug. 4. Sara, d. of John Tomlinson.
„   Aug. 12. Sarah, d. of Raph Morris.
„   Sept. 8. Margeret, d. of Raph Kendrick.
„   Oct. 18. Joyce, w. of Hugh Woodice.
„   Oct. 20. Margery, w. of John Tomlinson.
„   Oct. 24. Margery Yardley, wid.
„   Nov. 27. Francis Partrich.
„   Nov. 28. Kathren Hopkins, wid.
„   Dec. 14. A child of Lewes Rawley.
„   Dec. 16. Willm. Tomlinson *als.* Browne.
„   Dec. 26. Elizabeth Atkins, wid.
„   Dec. 30. A child of Willm. Blakemore, unbap.
163$\frac{5}{6}$, Jan. 4. Henrey Loe.
„   Mar. 14. Edward Key.
„   Mar. 19. Joyce, w. of Thomas Carlis.

ANNO DOMI., 1636.

1636, Mar. 28. Elizabeth Stanley.
„   Mar. 29. Elizabeth Fildust.
„   Apr. 2. Margery Thornton.
„   Apr. 23. Edward Sharpling.
„   May 29. Dorothy Edwards.
„   May 30. Margery Gadde.
„   June 18. Elizabeth Chatwin.
„   June 20. Infans Phillips, peregrina.
„   June 24. Francis & Gregory, ss. of Water Steeven.
„   July 3. Ann, d. of John Chetwin.
„   July 18. Simon Crowley.
„   July 28. Henry, s. of Henry Frith.
„   Aug. 3. Mary, d. of Richard Trantor.
„   Aug. 6. Edward Pearsons.
„   Aug. 21. Francis, s. of Richard Ashmore.

1636, Aug. 22.	Edward, s. of Thomas Heath.
„ Aug. 27.	Mrs. Margery Shilton.
„ Sept. 4.	Elnor, w. of Rape Kendrick.
„ Sept. 6.	Roland, s. of Roland Bett.
„ Sept. 15.	Ann Parsons, wid.
„ Sept. 21.	Francis Hawckes.
„ Sept. 21.	Jone, d. of Thomas Manton.
„ Sept. 22.	John, s. of Willm. Stanly.
„ Sept. 24.	Henry, s. of Henry Darby.
„ Sept. 27.	Thomas, s. of Thomas Atkis.
„ Oct. 16.	Francis, w. of Roger Chetwin.
„ Oct. 24.	Sarah, d. of John Parsons.
„ Nov. 7.	Mr. Thomas Johnson.
„ Nov. 21.	A s. of Mr. Willobey, unchris.
„ Nov. 22.	Sara, d. of John Round.
„ Dec. 1.	Henry, s. of Henry Wass.
„ Dec. 9.	A child of Richard Atkins, unchris.
„ Dec. 23.	Margeret Atkins.
163$\frac{6}{7}$, Jan. 12.	Robart, s. of Robart Rider.
„ Jan. 25.	A child of Willm. Chetwin, unchris.
„ Jan. 29.	Phillip Timins.
„ Feb. 9.	Margrey Jevens.
„ Feb. 13.	Raphe, s. of John Marsh.
„ Mar. 7.	Maudlin More, wid.
„ Mar. 24.	Jone, d. of George Partrich.

THOMAS GROVE,
JOHN BIRD,   } Economis.

1637.

1637, Mar. 26.	Thomas, s. of John Feild.
„ Mar. 27.	Willm. Dolphin.
„ Apr. 1.	Anne, d. of Thomas Frith.
„ Apr. 1.	Dina, d. of George Aplewis.
„ Apr. 29.	Isabell, d. of Thomas Chushmore.
„ June 28.	Richard Aire.
„ July 11.	Joseph Sharpling.
„ July 25.	Margoret Stery.
„ July 25.	Anne Mathewes.

1637, July 26. Judeth Hands.
  ,, Aug. 5. Nicolas Hands, Junr.
  ,, Aug. 6. Willm. Hands.
  ,, Aug. 10. Nicolas Hands, Senr.
  ,, Aug. 14. Elizabeth Setry.
  ,, Aug. 14. Willm. Dekin.
  ,, Sept. 9. Margeret Gill.
  ,, Sept. 15. John, s. of Edward Parsons.
  ,, Sept. 24. An Inft. of Francis Syncox, unbap.
  ,, Nov. 8. Margery, w. of Willm. James.
  ,, Dec. 10. Anna Hardwicke.
  ,, Dec. 24. Thomas Careles.
  ,, Dec. 25. Inft. of Willm. Marsh, unbap.
  ,, Dec. 29. Alice Wiley.
  ,, Dec. 27. Isabell, w. of Richard James.
  ,, Dec. 31. Walter Biley.
163⅞, Jan. 16. Isabell, w. of John Bond.
  ,, Jan. 22. Willm., s. of Anne Jesson.
  ,, Feb. 6. Alice, d. of Enward Traunter.
  ,, Mar. 18. Margeret, d. of Roger Smith.

THOMAS JESSON, ⎫
WILLM. STOORY, ⎬ Economis.

ANNO DOM., 1638.

1638, Apr. 10. Edward Reinolds.
  ,, Apr. 16. Paul Maier.
  ,, Apr. 24. Elizabeth Parsons *al.* Littley.
  ,, May 4. Willm. Careles.
  ,, May 23. William, s. of Henry Darby.
  ,, May 26. John, s. of William Reeves.
  ,, May 26. The unbap. child of John Marsh.
  ,, June 1. Thomas, s. of William Blakemore.
  ,, June 30. John Kirtland.
  ,, July 2. Willm. James *al.* Stringer.
  ,, July 11. Ann, w. of Roger Wright.
  ,, July 20. Thomason Wilye, wid.
  ,, July 24. Frances Briscoe.
  ,, Aug. 22. Sara, d. of Richard Ashmore.

1638, Sept. 30. The unbap. child of William & Isabell Hadley.
,, Oct. 10. Winifred Wilson.
,, Oct. 10. Thomas Church, of Barr.
,, Oct. 26. Ales Collier.
,, Nov. 18. Francis Byrd.
,, Dec. 8. Em, w. of William Parkes.
,, Dec. 15. Sara, w. of Willm. Johnson *al.* Wodham.
163$\frac{8}{9}$, Jan. 4. Sarah, d. of Willm. Sterry.
,, Jan. 9. John, s. of John & Mary Byrd.
,, Jan. 10. Margaret, w. of Robert Haywood.
,, Jan. 26. Jane Sabell, wid.
,, Jan. 28. Henry, s. of Thomas & Jane Cashmore.
,, Feb. 2. Unbap. child of Mary Herring, unlawfully begotten.
,, Mar. 12. Hughe, s. of George & Alice Basset.
,, Mar. 14. John Norris.

Anno Domi., 1639.

1639, Mar. 28. Rebecca, d. of William & Francis Richards.
,, May 13. Thomas Byrd.
,, May 13. Alice, w. of George Bassett.
,, Mar. 26. Elizabeth, w. of Gilbert Soaker.
,, Aug. 1. Edward Cole.
,, Aug. 10. John Reinolds.
,, Aug. 20. w. of William Guest.
,, Aug. 22. Ellonar, w. of John Rider.
,, Aug. 23. Henry Frith.
,, Aug. 25. The unbap. child of William Marsh.
,, Sept. 11. John Hewey.
,, Nov. 22. Elizabeth, d. of John Marsh.
163$\frac{9}{40}$, Feb. 6. Simeon Rider.
,, Feb. 22. Thomas Stoakes.
,, Mar. 4. Lucy, w. of Richard Hanson.
,, Mar. 6. John Wright.

Ano. Dm., 1640.

1640, Apr. 8. Alice, w. of Francis Syncox.
,, Apr. 10. Jone Asley.

1640, Apr. 20. Mary, w. of Henry Darby.

,, May 11. Katherine, d. of William & Anne Granger.

,, May 24. Katherine Loe, wid.

✓ ,, May 25. William Greene.

,, June 15. Georg Stanley.

,, July 3. The unbap. child of Richard Bird.

,, July 9. John Owen.

,, Aug. 4. Elizabeth Cox.

,, Aug. 4. Rebeccah, d. of John Ward.

,, Aug. 15. Elizabeth, w. of George Byrd.

,, Aug. 23. A child of Willm. & Winifreid Blackemore, unbap.

,, Aug. 27. Ellonar Filks.

,, Aug. 29. Barbara Wiersdale, wid.

,, Sept. 4. Timmozin Bennitte.

,, Sept. 5. William, s. of William Grice.

,, Sept. 12. Mary, w. of Richard Jones.

,, Sept. 20. Elizabeth, d. of William & Isabell Hadley.

,, Oct. 15. The unbap. child of William

,, Oct. 22. The unbap. child of Water Wiley.

,, Oct. 27. Anne, w. of Thomas Ockley.

,, Nov. 23. Thomas, s. of Thomas & Mary Gilbert.

,, Dec. 3. The unbap. child of Richard Ashmore.

,, Dec. 26. Elizabeth, w. of Richard Ashmore.

164$\frac{0}{1}$, Jan. 7. Kathren Hardick.

,, Jan. 7. A child of Edward Deeley.

,, Jan. 8. Unbap. child of Willm. Rowe.

,, Feb. 6. Mary, w. of William Turner.

,, Feb. 10. George Partrich.

,, Feb. 15. The unbap. child of John & Ellonar Ward.

✓ ,, Mar. 5. Elizabeth, w. of Thomas Heath.

,, Mar. 9. The s. of George & Mary Basset.

,, Mar. 12. Roger Hanson.

,, Mar. 16. Elizabeth, w. of Thomas Harley.

Anno Dmi., 1641.

1641, Apr. 4. Elizabeth, d. of Richard Cox.

,, Apr. 11. John, s. of Thomas & Margaret Dutton.

,, Apr. 30. Isabell, w. of William Tea.

1641, May   4. Thomas James *al*. Stringer.
  ,, June   1. The unbap. child of William & Winifred
                  Blakmore.
  ,, June   6. Isabell Ashley.
  ,, June   7. Mary, d. of Francis & Frances Edward.
  ,, June 10. Winifride, w. of William Blakmore.
  ,, June 14. Hugh, s. of Hugh & Elizabeth Merris.
  ,, Nov.   3. Nicholas Bridgin.
164½, Jan. 25. Richard, s. of Edward Hodgkins.
  ,, Jan.   26. Edward Groves.
  ,, Jan.   27. Richard Ashmore.
  ,, Mar.   3. Jane, w. of John Stanley.
  ,, Mar. 16. John Salt.
✓ ,, Mar. 18. Isaak Hall.

Anno Dmi., 1642.

1642, May 11. Raph, s. of John & Margaret Marsh.
  ,, June   1. Elizabeth, d. of Francis Edwards.
  ,, June   1. William Bull.
✓ ,, June 19. Alice Greene.
  ,, July 12. Mary, d. of William Chadwin.
7 ⌐ ,, July 20. Jone Wright.
  ,, July 23. Lettice, w. of Sir Richard Shilton, Knt.
  ,, July 24. Elizabeth Pope.
⌐ ,, July 27. Richard Wright.
  ,, Aug.   9. The unbap. child of William Fildust.
  ,, Aug. 15. Alice Chatwin.
  ,, Aug. 25. William, s. of George & Mary Robsart.
  ,, Aug. 25. The unbap. child of George Robsart.
  ,, Sept. 20. William, s. of William Granger.
  ,, Nov.   3. William, s. of Edward Dudley.
⌐ ,, Nov. 13. Ellonar, d. of John Brooks.   7
  ,, Nov. 14. Dorothie Owen.
  ,, Dec.   4. William Dudley.
  ,, Dec.   5. Jone Partrich.
  ,, Dec. 22. Robert Blakiley.
164⅔, Jan.   3. Sara, d. of Richard Bird.
  ,, Jan.   6. Elizabeth Penne.
  ,, Jan. 19. Henry Jarvis.

164⅔, Jan. 22. Jane Wood.

„   Feb. 11. Ursilah Ockley.

„   Feb. 11. William Stanley.

„   Feb. 21. The w. of John Tomson, of Ldbery.

„   Mar. 5. William Osborn.

„   Mar. 14. A child of Richard James, unbap.

1643.

1643, Apr. 4. The child of Edward Fenton, unbap.

„   Apr. 8. The w. of Thomas Leese.

„   Apr. 10. Willm. Granger.

„   Apr. 14. Ellinor Smith, of Smethwicke.

„   May 6. John More.

„   May 8. Alce Hadley.

„   May 22. Willm. Bird.

„   May 24. George Partrich.

„   May 30. Willm. Partrich.

„   June 13. Sarah Grove.

„   June 21. Isabell Osborne.

„   July 9. Jane Partrich.

„   July 11. John Chetwin.

„   July 12. John Renolds.

„   Sept. 8. A child of John Beedonson.

„   Sept. 9. Richard Bird.

„   Sept. 15. Elizabeth Gilbart.

„   Sept. 17. John Parsons.

„   Sept. 27. Water Orris.

„   Nov. 13. Elizabeth Jones.

„   Nov. 20. William Hall.

„   Nov. 23. Margery Cashmore.

„   Dec. 13. Elizabeth, d. of Robart Turnor.

164¾, Jan. 7. Thomas Drewry.

„   Jan. 11. A child of George Jesson.

„   Jan. 22. Gilbert Stoker.

„   Jan. 27. Raph Reve.

„   Jan. 30. Hendry Cole.

„   Feb. 3. Philip Halbons.

„   Feb. 3. Eliner Wockley.

„   Feb. 11. Alce Dudley.

1644¾,	Mar.	17.	Sifley Nevill.
,,	Mar.	20.	Willm. Forme.
,,	Mar.	24.	Issabell Partrich.
1644,	Mar.	25.	Izacke Stanton.
,,	May	12.	Elizabeth Bird.
,,	May	12.	John Wright.
,,	May	13.	Willm. Bird.
,,	May	17.	Thomas Grove.
,,	May	17.	Mary Rawley.
,,	June	19.	William Gest
,,	June	30.	Richard Reding.
,,	July	8.	Ann Gretton.
,,	July	11.	Elinor Wall.
,,	July	19.	John Sabin.
✓ ,,	Aug.	5.	Roger Wright.
,,	Aug.	10.	Edward Stanton.
,,	Aug.	23.	George Addams.
,,	Sept.	10.	Alce Salt.
,,	Sept.	10.	A child of Edward Rider, unbap.
,,	Sept.	15.	Elizabeth Feild.
,,	Oct.	4.	Jone Cooke.
,,	Nov.	15.	Hanna Aughton.
,,	Nov.	16.	John Curtler.
,,	Dec.	6.	A base born child of Jone Tailor's.
✓ ,,	Dec.	16.	Ann Hall.
,,	Dec.	19.	William Tey.
,,	Dec.	19.	William Sincox.
,,	Dec.	23.	Michaell Sincox.
1644⅘,	Jan.	4.	Jane Stanley.
,,	Jan.	7.	Ann Dekon.
,,	Jan.	7.	Hugh Harper.
,,	Jan.	10.	Ann Ensworth.
,,	Jan.	11.	John Avans.
,,	Jan.	20.	Frances Perkin.
,,	Jan.	23.	Alice Laud.
,,	Jan.	27.	Alec, w. of John Morris.
,,	Jan.	29.	Jone Newhey.
,,	Feb.	10.	Frances Turton.
,,	Feb.	27.	Alce Timins.

1644⅘, Mar. 5.   Ann Blackhorn.
„ Mar. 23.   Jone Hides.

1645.

1645, Mar. 27.   Dorothy Stanton.
„ Apr. 16.   Mary Orris.
„ Apr. 21.   Thomas Jonsson.
„ Apr. 23.   Grace, the soposed d. of Edward Cole.
„ Apr. 26.   A child of John Bird, of the Horton Way.
„ Apr. 29.   John Woodward.
„ May 2.   Mary, d. of a poore wooman.
„ May 4.   Elizabeth Bird.
„ May 12.   Joyce Cope.
„ May 16.   Margret Caley.
„ June 13.   Richard Clemson.
„ June 20.   Richard Wile.
„ June 20.   Margret Cartwright.
„ June 27.   Elinor Carles.
„ July 6.   Elizabeth, d. of Thomas Atkins.
„ Aug. 16.   Jone, d. of John Atkins.
„ Aug. 19.   Elizabeth, d. of John Salt.
„ Aug. 24.   Mary Baker.
„ Sept. 2.   Abigall, d. of John Atkins.
„ Sept. 3.   Mary, d. of Richard Jones.
„ Sept. 10.   Elizabeth Wall, of Oldbury.
„ Sept. 15.   Mary Vale and her child, unbap.
„ Sept. 25.   Jone Partrich.
„ Oct. 2.   Elizabeth Wall.
„ Oct. 3.   Alce Salt.
„ Oct. 30.   Penelope Jones.
„ Nov. 12.   Alce, w. of Grifyhin Orme.
„ Nov. 19.   [*omitted*], w. of John Hanson.
„ Nov. 30.   George Aplewes.
„ Nov. 30.   Simon Yonge.
„ Dec. 3.   Margret Greene, wid.
1644⅚, Jan. 14.   Willm., s. of William Wall.
„ Jan. 14.   Thomas Turton.
„ Jan. 16.   Simon Sincoxe.
„ Jan. 23.   John Cam.

164$\frac{5}{6}$, Feb. 9.   Mary Tranter.
  ,,   Feb. 14.   William Dawson.
  ,,   Mar. 1.   John Cooke.
  ,,   Mar. 2.   Edward, s. of Willm. Blackmore.
  ,,   Mar. 20.   Edmond Wiley.

1646.

1646, Mar. 25.   The wid. Renolds.
  ,,   Apr. 27.   Lewes Rawley.
  ,,   May   2.   John Benet.
  ,,   May   5.   Ann Kendrick.
  ,,   May   8.   Thomas Leghe.
  ,,   May   8.   Elinor Renoles.
  ,,   June 2.   Francis Wiersdale.
  ,,   June 4.   Judeth Renolds.
  ,,   June 4.   Margret Dudley.
  ,,   June 8.   Water Orris.
  ,,   June 10.   Jone Best.
  ,,   June 20.   Robart Rider.
  ,,   Aug. 12.   William, s. of John Renoles
  ,,   Aug. 27.   William Sterrey.
  ,,   Sept. 17.   Jone Davis.
  ,,   Nov. 5.   Willm. Allen.
✓ ,,   Dec. 17.   Christopher Greene.
  ,,   Dec. 18.   Mary Tranter.
164$\frac{6}{7}$, Jan. 23.   Joseph Atkins.
  ,,   Feb. 14.   There was one of Darleston.
  ,,   Feb. 23.   The wid. Cleaton.
  ,,   Mar. 1.   Mary Dudley.
  ,,   Mar. 15.   [*omitted*], s. of Water Stevens, Junr.

1647.

1647, Mar. 27.   Jane, d. of Thomas Cashmore, Junr.
  ,,   June 1.   Mary, w. of Richard Parkes.
  ,,   June 4.   Anne, w. of John Turton.
  ,,   June 5.   Edward Pincard.
  ,,   May 18.   Mary Parks.
  ,,   June 2.   Amey Turton.

1647, June 21.　Thomas Granger.
　,,　June 22.　Margret Deeley.
　,,　June 23.　John Hanson.
　,,　June 27.　Margery Atkins.
　,,　July 30.　Elizabeth Jarvis.
　,,　Aug. 16.　William Richards.
　,,　Aug. 17.　Thomas Blackham.
　,,　Nov. 3.　Ann Grise.
　,,　Nov. 5.　Ann Bidle.
　,,　Nov. 19.　Thomas Renoles.
　,,　Nov. 22.　Georg Woodward.
　,,　Nov. 23.　Willm. Taylor.
　,,　Nov. 25.　Robert Wiliams.
　,,　Dec. 6.　John Hurst.
　,,　Dec. 7.　Sir Richard Shelton, Knyght.
　,,　Dec. 15.　Margery Sincox.
164⅞, Jan. 6.　Dorothy Bankes.
　,,　Jan. 10.　Sifley Haywood.
　,,　Jan. 16.　John Best.
　,,　Jan. 17.　Mary Round, of Oldbery.
　,,　Jan. 22.　A child of George Robin's.
　,,　Feb. 6.　Elizabeth Partrich.
　,,　Feb. 7.　Katheren Jesson.
　,,　Feb. 17.　John Coley.
　,,　Mar. 12.　Thomas Gelbart.
　,,　Mar. 13.　Thomas Grove.
　,,　Mar. 16.　John Callam.
　,,　Mar. 20.　Richard Dudley.

1648.

1648, Mar. 29.　John Sincox.
　,,　Apr. 30.　John Ward.
　,,　May 4.　Elizabeth Orris.
　,,　June 5.　Richard, s. of Raph Wotton.
　,,　June 7.　Susan Stanley.
　,,　June 15.　The unbap. child of Thomas Cashmore.
　,,　June 16.　Elizabeth, d. of Henry Edwards.
√　,,　June 20.　John Brooke.
　,,　July 23.　Elizabeth, d. of John Orris.

1648,	Aug.	1.	Katheren Wasse.
,,	Aug.	6.	Thomas, s. of Willm. Partrich.
,,	Aug.	24.	William Deeley, of Oldberry.
,,	Oct.	5.	Elizabeth Jarvis.
,,	Nov.	12.	William Carles.
,,	Nov.	26.	Ann Pearsall.
,,	Dec.	5.	William Tibots.
,,	Dec.	6.	Thomas Woodward.
,,	Dec.	7.	Sarah, w. of Alexander Loe.
164$\frac{8}{9}$,	Jan.	24.	John Turton.
,,	Jan.	24.	An unbap. child of William Wiley.
,,	Feb.	5.	Jane Marsh.
,,	Feb.	12.	Alce, d. of William Fildust.
,,	Feb.	16.	[*omitted*], d. of Edward Sincox.
,,	Feb.	21.	Alce Gadd.
,,	Feb.	21.	John Parsons.
,,	Feb.	25.	Richard Jones.
,,	Mar.	4.	Richard Henley.
,,	Mar.	7.	Richard, s. of John Partrich.
,,	Mar.	10.	Francis Wiersdale.

1649.

1649,	Apr.	26.	Alce, d. of Thomas Reed.
,,	Apr.	28.	Ann Rider.
,,	Apr.	30.	Hendry Duger.
,,	May	4.	Thomas, s. of Isake Fildust.
,,	May	16.	Ann Jarvis.
,,	May	27.	Ann Darbey & an unbap. child.
,,	May	27.	Sara Bird.
,,	June	3.	Joyce, d. of Thomas Fryth.
,,	June	4.	William Woodward.
,,	June	19.	Mrs. Mary, w. of Mr. John Shelton, Esquier.
,,	June	27.	Sara, d. of Alexander Woodward.
,,	July	6.	Elizabeth, d. of Robart Marsh.
,,	July	19.	Alce, w. of John Osborne.
,,	July	22.	Sara, d. of Alexander Woodward.
,,	Aug.	16.	Mary Fenton.
,,	Aug.	18.	Edward Lidiat.
,,	Aug.	18.	Joseph, s. of Thomas Jesson.

1649, Sept. 10. Raphe Marsh.
  ,, Nov. 20. Elizabeth Poltney.
  ,, Nov. 26. John Sincox.
  ,, Dec. 1. Mary Dudley.
  ,, Dec. 24. Walter Stevens.
164$\frac{49}{50}$, Jan. 16. The unbap. child of John Edwards
  ,, Jan. 18. Richard Woodward.
  ,, Feb. 14. William Bird.
  ,, Feb. 27. Alexander Jarvis.
  ,, Feb. 22. Edward Diall.
  ,, Mar. 7. Richard, s. of Thomas Jesson.
  ,, Mar. 8. Kathren Wright.
  ,, Mar. 8. Jefferey Cooke.
  ,, Mar. 11. Francis Hoggets.
  ,, Mar. 18. Elinor Large.

1650.

1650, Mar. 29. Ann, d. of John Stokes.
  ,, Mar. 29. Mary, d. of Thomas Dutton.
  ,, Mar. 31. Edithe Wiley.
  ,, Apr. 16. Elizabeth Wiersdale.
  ,, May 21. Ann, d. of Thomas Sincox.
  ,, Aug. 7. Margeret Cox.
  ,, Aug. 11. William Chetwind.
  ,, Aug. 17. George, s. of William Partrich.
  ,, Aug. 25. Jone Tymins.
  ,, Aug. 28. John, s. of John Baker.
  ,, Oct. 7. John Hall.
  ,, Oct. 27. Thomas Gilbert.
  ,, Nov. 20. Elizabeth Wiley.
  ,, Nov. 26. Elizabeth Atkins.
  ,, Dec. 3. George Sincox, Naylor.
  ,, Dec. 6. Edward Smith, of Smethwick.
  ,, Dec. 30. Elizabeth, w. of William Wily.
165$\frac{0}{1}$, Jan. 10. Thomas Simcox.
  ,, Jan. 27. William Wiley, [*erased*].
  ,, Jan. 27. William Wily, Clarke.
  ,, Mar. 16. Richard Partrigh.
  ,, Mar. 20. William Martin.
  ,, Mar. 22. Richard Spury.

Anno Domini, 1651.

1651, June 4. William Shelgilt.
  ,, June 28. William Grice.
  ,, Aug. 10. Mary Woodward.
  ,, Aug. 20. John Orris.
165½, Jan. 16. Ann Fildust.
  ,, Jan. 26. Jone Edwards.
  ,, Feb. 6. Jone Dutton.
  ,, Feb. 20. Thomas Dutton.

1653. Baptisms. Vol. II.

1653, Oct. 2. Mary, d. of Anthony & Ruth Evans, Naylor.
      John, s. of John & Mary Baker, Naylor, was
      borne the same day.
  ,, Oct. 18. William, s. of Isacke & Mary Filders, Naylor.
  ,, Oct. 15. Ellinor, d. of Samuel &   Hopkisse,
      Naylor.
  ,, Oct. 20. Elizabeth, d. of   & Ann Bennet,
      Bucklemaker.
  ,, Oct. 28. John, s. of Thomas & Anne Hadley, Naylor.
  ,, Nov. 7. John, s. of Edward & Ellenor White, Black-
      smith.
  ,, Nov. 21. Samuel, s. of Thomas & Mary Jesson, Yeo-
      man.
  ,, Nov. 22. John, s. of Henry & Ann Medhurst, Chapman.
  ,, Nov. 23. Thomas, s. of Thomas & Ellinor Bird,
      Carpenter.
  ,, Dec. 9. Mary, d. of William & [*illegible*] Bird,
      Carpenter.
  ,, Dec. 10. Richard, s. of John & Ann Bird, Naylor.
  ,, Dec. 12. John & Thomas, ss. of William & Ann
      Blakemore, Naylor.
  ,, Dec. 17. Walter, s. of Walter & Elizabeth [*illegible*],
      Naylor.
165¾, Jan. 6. Jane, d. of Nicholas & Elizabeth Jury,
      Naylor.
  ,, Jan. 18. Anne, d. of Richard & Mary [*illegible*].
  ,, Jan. 22. Mary, d. of Robert & [*illegible*], Naylor.

1655¾, Feb. 4. Henry, s. of Isack & Jane Hull, Naylor.

,, Feb. 7. Sarah, d. of Thomas & Anne Large, Naylor.

,, Feb. 13. Samuel, s. of Roger & Susan Griffin, Sawyer.
Elizabeth, d. of John [*illegible*].

,, Feb. 17. Mary, d. of Robert & Frances Bate, Naylor.

,, Feb. 20. John, s. of Alexander & Mary Hawkes,
Naylor.

,, Feb. 22. Mary, d. of John & Jane Cole, Naylor.

,, Feb. 27. Charles, s. of John & Margaret Cox, Taylur.

,, Feb. 27. John, s. of Edward & Sarah Cole, Naylor.

,, Mar. 1. John, s. of John & Mary Butler, Ironmonger.

,, Mar. 6. Mary, d. of Richard & Mary Atkisse, Naylor.

,, Mar. 7. Mary, d. of Thomas & Ann Ashmore, Naylor.

,, Mar. 11. Ellenor, d. of Francis & Alce Hinkinson,
Naylor.

,, Mar. 12. Hanna, d. of Edward & Mary Dudley,
Cooper.

,, Mar. 14. John, s. of John & Hannah Cashmore,
Naylor.

,, Mar. 20. John, s. of Francis & Sarah Reeves, Naylor.

1654, Mar. 30. Elizabeth, d. of Mr. John Shelton, Esq.
&

,, Apr. 6. Anne, d. of Samuel & Ellinor Hickin,
Butcher.

,, Apr. 6, Thomas, s. of John & Alse Baker, Mason.

,, Apr. 8. Samuell, s. of Richard & Isabell Collins,
Naylor.

,, Apr. 22. John, s. of Thomas & Elizabeth Simcox,
husbandman.

,, May 2. Anne, d. of William & Ellenor Reeve, Naylor.

,, May 18. Elizabeth, d. of John & Elizabeth Cox,
Laborer.

,, May 29. John, s. of Henry & Mary Vale, hbdman.

,, June 11. Elizabeth, d. of Richard & Mary Jesson,
Yeoman.

,, June 21. Mary, d. of Henry & Mary Avory.

,, July 1. Edward, s. of Thomas & Mary Frith, Weaver.

,, July 10. Jane, d. of Thomas & Elizabeth Michell,
Naylor.

1654, July 24. Thomas, s. of Edward Hill, Naylor.
„ Aug. 3. John, s. of Samuel & Jane Firkin, Naylor.
„ Aug. 8. Mary, d. of Thomas & Unite Priest, Hbdman.
„ Aug. 10. Abigall, d. of William Bury.
„ Aug. 10. Roberte, d. of John & Abigall Simcox, Yeoman.
„ Aug. 16. William, s. of Thomas & Mary Tunkes, Naylor.
„ Aug. 23. John, s. of John & Margaret Hawkes, Yeoman
„ Sept. 25. Samuel, s. of Richard Robinson, Naylor.
„ Oct. 4. William, s. of Raphe & Elizabeth Kendrick, Naylor.
„ Oct. 8. Sarah, d. of Mr. William Turton, of the Oke, & Sarah, his wife.
„ Oct. 9. Elizabeth, d. of Edward & Dorothy Burges, Naylor.
„ Oct. 10. Humfrey, s. of Humfrey & Jone Dudley, Naylor.
„ Oct. 10. Nicholas, s. of Nicholas & Elizabeth Okeley, Naylor.
„ Oct. 12. Mary, d. of Francis & Jane Heath, Bucklemaker.
„ Oct. 24. Richard, s. of John & Mary Boyer, laborer.
„ Nov. 12. Robert, s. of Robert & Alse Turnor, weaver.
„ Nov. 20. Priscilla, d. of Thomas & Ann Stokes, Naylor.
„ Dec. 16. Raphe, s. of Raphe & Katherine Stanley, Naylor.
„ Dec. 30. Elizabeth, d. of William & Anne Wiley, Bucklemaker.
165⅘, Jan. 20. Mary, d. of John & Mary Bate, Naylor.
„ Jan. 20. Mary, d. of Francis & Elizabeth Liddiatt, Naylor.
„ Jan. 21. Elizabeth, d. of William & Katheren White, Lab.
„ Jan. 22. Henry, s. of Thomas & Jone Stanley, Taylor.
„ Jan. 22. Edward, s. of Thomas & Elizabeth Morris, Smith.
„ Feb. 3. Richard, s. of Edward & Sarah Dudley, Butcher.

165⅘, Feb. 3. Joseph, s. of Robert & Anne Turner, Nayler.

,, Feb. 6. John, s. of John & Mary Ward, Nayler.

,, Feb. 22. John, s. of John & Anne Kelham.

,, Feb. 26. Thomas, s. of Robert & Mary Mearihurst, Naylor.

,, Feb. 27. Richard, s. of William & Elizabeth Bird, Naylor.

,, Mar. 13. Roger, s. of Roger & Mary Colborne.

1655, Apr. 1. Sarah, d. of William & Anne Tunkes, Nayler.

,, Apr. 15. John, s. of John & Elizabeth Preston, Naylor.

,, Apr. 25. Margaret, d. of Richard & Elizabeth Carelesse, Baker.

,, Apr. 30. Cornelius, s. of George & Mary Jesson, Yeoman.

,, May 8. Mary, d. of George & Dorothy Marsh, Bucklemaker.

,, May 16. Sibbill, d. of Mr. John Shilton, Esq., & Elizabeth, his wife.

,, May 20. William, s. of John & Allse Baker, Carpenter.

,, June 8. Jone, d. of Samuel & Ellinor Hopkins, Naylor.

,, June 11. Joseph, s. of John & Margery Hinton, Lab.

,, June 24. Richard, s. of Richard & Ellenor Woodward, Naylor.

,, July 2. Richard, s. of Richard & Mary Parks, Naylor.

,, July 4. Randall, s. of John & Mary Robinson.

,, July 7. Hanna & Anne, ds. of John & Mary Bird, Naylor.

,, July 8. John, s. of John & Anne Deeley, Naylor.

,, July 10. Elizabeth, d. of Thomas & Mary Jesson, Yeoman.

,, July 24. Sarah, d. of Thomas & Alse Lambe, Naylor.

,, Aug. 20. John, s. of John & Margery Riley, Naylor.

,, Aug. 31. Katherine, d. of Thomas & Alse Reed, Warriner.

,, Sept. 7. Sarah, d. of Richard & Mary Atkisse, Naylor.

,, Sept. 8. Mary, d. of John & Alse Cartwright, Naylor.

,, Oct. 6. Mary, d. of Thomas & Mary Gilbert, Naylor.

1655, Oct. 8. Humfrey, s. of Isack & Jane Hall, Naylor. ✓ *l l*

„ Oct. 12. Elizabeth, d. of Thomas & Jane Bayley, Naylor.

„ Oct. 12. Jobe, s. of Michael & Elizabeth Simcox.

„ Oct. 13. John, s. of John & Alse Kendrick, Naylor.

„ Oct. 13. Sarah, d. of Joseph & Sarah Bond, Naylor.

„ Oct. 16. William, s. of John & Mary Butler, Ironmonger.

„ Oct. 16. Richard, s. of Richard & Alse Sterry, of the Swanne.

„ Oct. 17. Sarah, d. of Thomas & Joane Cashmore, Naylor.

„ Oct. 24. Edward, s. of Richard & Jone Brookes, Lab.

„ Nov. 4. Thomas, s. of Thomas & Alse Large, Naylor.

„ Nov. 5. William, s. of John & Margery Jones, Naylor.

„ Nov. 8. Joseph, s. of Henry Bowman, Firemaker.

„ Nov. 11. Anne, d. of John & Anne Hall, Naylor. *r*

„ Dec. 2. Thomas, s. of Thomas & Margaret Kendricke.

165⅚, Jan. 1. Martha, d. of Richard & Mary Jesson, Yeoman.

„ Jan. 1. John, s. of Gregory & Katharine Evans, Naylor.

„ Jan. 5. Mary, d. of Alezander & Mary Hawkes, Naylor.

„ Jan. 11. John, s. of Robert & Joane Stanley.

„ Feb. 6. William, s. of John & Elizabeth Stokes, Naylor.

„ Feb. 9. John, s. of Raphe & Elizabeth Culwicke, Bucklemaker.

„ Feb. 17. Sarah, d. of Edward & Mary Simcox, Naylor.

„ Feb. 17. Thomas, s. of Barbara Stowe. This son of Barbara Stowe was unlawfully begotten by Isaak Hall.

„ Feb. 19. Mary, d. of Thomas & Anne Hadley, Naylor.

1656, Mar. 29. Thomas, s. of Edward & Anne Hawkes, Kidder.

„ Apr. 5. Margaret, d. of William & Anne Cox, Naylor.
Ann, d. of John Gad, was bapt. May 25th, 1655.

1656, Apr. 17.   Jane, d. of Isake & Mary Filders.

,,   Apr. 19.   Mary, d. of Roger & Susanna Griffith, Sawyer.

,,   Apr. 22.   Phebe, d. of Mr. John Shilton & Elizabeth, his wife.

,,   Apr. 28.   Sarah, d. of Henry & Margery Wasse.

,,   May 10.   George, s. of John & Margaret Cox, Taylor.

,,   June 15.   Sarah, d. of William & Ellenor Reeves, Naylor.

,,   June 18.   John, s. of Mr. William Turton, of the Oke, & Sarah, his wife.

,,   June 20.   Robert, s. of Robert & Alse Turnor, Weaver.

,,   June 25.   Abraham, s. of Francis & Anne Thornton, Naylor.

,,   June 29.   Hanna, d. of Thomas & Mary Atkisse, Naylor.

,,   July 1.   Mary, d. of Thomas & Katharine Sault, Mason.

,,   July 15.   Joseph, s. of John & Jone Atkisse, Naylor.

,,   Aug. 4.   Richard, s. of Thomas & Mary Tunkes.

,,   Aug. 11.   Mary, d. of John & Anne Deeley, Naylor.

,,   Aug. 30.   Jobe, s. of Francis & Dorcas Morris, Naylor.

,,   Sept. 8.   Elizabeth, d. of Richard & Elizabeth Cox, Labourer.

,,   Sept. 19.   Joseph, s. of Richard & Margery Wheeler.

,,   Sept. 21.   John, s. of John & Alse Baker, Mason.

,,   Sept. 26.   Edward, s. of Roger & Ellinor Southall, Naylor.

,,   Sept. 27.   Elizabeth, d. of John & Hanna Cashmore, Naylor.

,,   Oct. 2.   Ellenor, d. of Thomas Bird, Joyner, & another daughter, buried unbaptised, both born same day.

,,   Oct. 28.   Ellenor, d. of Nicholas & Elizabeth Jury, Naylor.

,,   Nov. 23.   Elizabeth, d. of John & Mary Bate, Naylor.

,,   Nov. 30.   Josias, s. of Richard & Mary Parkes, Naylor.

,,   Dec. 1.   John, s. of John & Ellinor Harvy.

,,   Dec. 13.   John, s. of John & Priscilla Lowe, Ironmonger.

1656, Dec. 14. Anne, d. of Robert & Anne Marsh, Bucklemaker.

„ Dec. 15. Mary, d. of Nicholas & Jane Hodgkins,
Taylor.

„ Dec. 16. Thomas, s. of Samuell & Ellinor Hopkins,
Naylor.

„ Dec. 21. Martha, d. of Henry & Mary Avory, of the
Rodmill.

165$\frac{6}{7}$, Jan. 9. Margery, d. of Nicholas & Joane Wyley.

„ Jan. 11. Elizabeth, d. of Walter & Elizabeth Fenton,
Naylor.

„ Jan. 13. Katharine, d. of William & Lovey Bird,
Carpenter.

„ Jan. 20. Francis, s. of Francis & Elizabeth Hawkes,
Naylor.

„ Jan. 22. Margaret, d. of Richard & Margaret Atkisse,
Naylor.

„ Jan. 24. John, s. of John & Jane Cole, Naylor.

„ Feb. 11. Richard, s. of Joseph & Mary Smith, Blacksmith.

„ Feb. 13. Sarah, d. of Edward & Sarah Cole, Naylor.

„ Feb. 13. Eva, d. of Edward & Dorothy Burges,
Naylor.

„ Feb. 14. William, s. of John & Margaret Hawkes,
Yeoman.

„ Feb. 15. Ellenor, d. of Richard & Ellenor Woodward,
Naylor.

„ Feb. 21. John, s. of Humphrey & Jane Dudley,
Naylor.

„ Mar. 6. Sarah, d. of Thomas & Margery Brookes,
servant to Mr. John Shilton.

„ Mar. 13. Mary, d. of William & Elizabeth Johnson,
Naylor.

„ Mar. 13. Jane, d. of Richard & Mary Tranter, Naylor.

„ Mar. 23. Margery, d. of John & Margery Jones,
Naylor.

1657, Apr. 11. Elizabeth, d. of Raphe & Elizabeth Wotton,
Labourer.

„ Apr. 20. Anne, d. of John & Mary Kirtland, phisitian.

1657, May 1. Paull, s. of John & Elizabeth Edwards, Naylor.

,, May 6. Thomas, s. of Thomas & Anne Stokes, Naylor.

,, May 13. William, s. of Raphell & Margaret Avory, of the Rodmell.

,, May 26. Bartholomew, s. of William & Anne Wiley, Bucklemaker.

,, June 12. Hanna, d. of John & Mary Robinson.

,, July 3. Joseph, s. of Richard & Mary Atkisse, Naylor.

,, July 3. Daniell, s. of John & Anne Kelham, Cole-carier.

,, July 4. Sarah, d. of William & Mary Bird, Naylor.

,, July 7. Walter, s. of Frances Kendricke, unlawfully begotten.

,, Aug. 14. Ephraim, s. of Robert & Anne Turnor.

,, Aug. 16. William, s. of William & Anne Smith, Bucklemaker.

,, Aug. 20. John, s. of Thomas & Anne Ashinor, Naylor.

,, Aug. 22. Mary, d. of Richard & Alse Wright.

,, Aug. 23. Edward, s. of Edward & Dorothy Bikur.

,, Sept. 6. Joseph, s. of William & Katharine White, Laborer.

,, [omitted.] Mary, d. of John & Margery Hinton, Laborer.

,, Oct. 17. Margery, d. of Thomas & Isabell Mayou.

,, Oct. 28. John, s. of John & Hanna Mayou, Weaver.

,, Nov. 10. Thomas, s. of Richard & Jone Brooks, Laborer.

,, Nov. 24. John, s. of Richard Robinson.

,, Nov. 25. Anne, d. of Thomas & Elizabeth Simcox, Husbandman.

,, Dec. 3. Elizabeth, d. of Thomas Browne, Huntsman.

,, Dec. 18. Jobe, s. of Thomas & Joane Stanley, Taylor.

,, Dec. 19. Alse, d. of Richard & Alse Stirry, Inholder.

,, Dec. 20. John, s. of Francis & Alse Hinkinson, Naylor.

,, Dec. 24. Elizabeth, d. of Francis & Elizabeth Hawkes.

165⅞, Jan. 4. Mary, d. of John & Anne Edwards, Naylor.

,, Jan. 15. George, s. of William Burges, Taylor.

165⅞, Jan. 22. William, s. of Robert Stanley, Naylor.

  ,,   Feb. 5. John, s. of Joseph & Margery Broome, Naylor.

  ,,   Feb. 25. Edward, s. of John & Anne Taylor, Naylor.

  ,,   Mar. 8. Mary, d. of Samuell White.

  ,,   Mar. 13. Paull, s. of John & Margaret Cox, Taylor.

  ,,   Mar. 13. Sarah, d. of William & Elizabeth Johnson, Naylor.

1658, Apr. 2. John, s. of John Cartwright.

  ,,   Apr. 11. Ellenor & Sarah, ds. of Francis Liddiatt.

  ,,   William, s. of Thomas Bird, Carpenter.

  ,,   Ephraim, s. of Roger & Mar. Colborne.

  ,,   May 20. Rebecka, d. of Francis &   Poultney, Husbandman.

  ,,   June 3. Amy, d. of Richard & Katharine Underhill.

  ,,   June 4. Margery, d. of Michaell & Elizabeth Simcox, Naylor.

  ,,   June 10. Mary & Martha, ds. of Thomas & Alse [*torn out*].

  ,,   June 11. Anne, d. of Joseph & Elizabeth Johnson, Naylor.

  ,,   June 24. Mary, d. of William Taylor, Naylor.

  ,,   July 20. Mary, d. of Richard Carelesse, Baker.

  ,,   July 25. Sarah, d. of Thomas & Margaret Kendricke.

  ,,   Aug. 20. John, s. of Joseph & Hanna Morris.

  ,,   Aug. 25. Mary, d. of Richard & Guendalene Gretton.

  ,,   Aug. 30. Richard, s. of Raphe Wotton.

  ,,   Sept. 15. Elizabeth, d. of Richard & Mary Shinton, Naylor.

  ,,   of Thomas & Anne Hadley.

  ,,   Sept. 30. of John Ward, Naylor.

  ,,   Oct. 23. Edward, s. of Edward & Margery Trantor.

  ,,   Oct. 26. William, s. of Edward & Margery Smith, Warrenor.

  ,,   Oct. 28. Mary, d. of Humfrey & Elizabeth Case, Gardner.

  ,,   Nov. 15. Jane, d. of Thomas &   Cashmore, Naylor.

  ,,   Nov. 29. Alexander, s. of John & Prissilla Lowe, Ironmonger.

1658, Dec. 15. Jane, d. of John & Hanna Cashmore, Naylor.

,, Dec. 22. Joseph, s. of George Marsh.

,, Dec. 22.   s. of George Marsh, Bucklemaker.

,,   of Thomas Stokes, Naylor.

,,   of Francis & Dorkas Morris, Naylor.

165 8/9, Jan. 1.   s. of Henry & Margery Wasse, Laborer.

,, Jan. 19.   d. of William & Ellenor Reeves, Naylor.

,, Jan.   d. of John & Jane Hadley, Naylor.

,, Jan. 21. Samuell, s. of Joseph & Sarah Bond, Naylor.

,, Feb. 20. Joseph, s. of John & Alse Baker, Mason.

3 √   ,, Feb. 22. Anne, d. of Isake & Jane Hall, Naylor.

,, Feb. 27. Samuell, s. of William Traford, of the forge.

,,   Mary, d. of William & Anne Smith, Bucklemaker.

,, Mar. 5. Sarah, d. of George & Margaret White, Bucklemaker.

,, Mar. 14.   s. of Thomas Sault.

,, Mar. 16. Alse, d. of James Cox, Victueler.

3   √   ,, Mar. 19. William, s. of Thomas Brooks.

,, Mar. 20. Moses, s. of Gregory & Katharine Evans, Naylor.

,, Mar. 21. Richard, s. of Mr. John & Mary Butler, Ironmonger.

,, Mar. 22. John, s. of Robert Turnor, Weaver.

1659, Mar. 28. Sarah, d. of George & Mary Jesson.

,, Apr. 9. Anne, d. of Thomas & Anne Frith.

,, Apr. 17. Mary, d. of Henry Frith, Naylor.

√   ,, Apr. 27. Isake, s. of John &   Hall, Naylor.

,, May 24. Elizabeth, d. of Mr. William & Sarah Turton.

,, May 25. Mary, d. of William Steevens.

,,   of William Blakemore.

,, June 10. Margaret, d. of John &   Jones, Naylor.

,, June 18. William, s. of Raphe & E. Culwicke, Naylor.

,,   of Isake & Mary Filders, Cobler.

,,   of William &   France.

,, June 29. Sarah, d. of Richard Robinson *alias* Mason.

,, July 22. John, s. of John Shilton, Esquire, & Elizabeth, his wyfe.

1859, Aug. 21. Thomas, s. of Thomas Carelesse.
  ,, Aug. 23. Francis, s. of Henry Penne, Naylor.
  ,, Aug. 24. Moses, s. of Humfrey Dudley, Naylor.
  ,, Aug. 24. Richard, s. of Richard Underhill.
  ,, [omitted].   of Francis & Dorkas Morris.
  ,, Sept. 4. John, s. of Henry Frith, of Sandwell.
  ,, Sept. 17. Edward, s. of John Mandicke, Naylor.
  ,, Sept. 20. Edward, s. of Thomas Trantor, Naylor.
  ,, [omitted].   of Samuel &   Hickin, Butcher.
  ,, [omitted].   of John & [Hannah ?] Mayo, Weaver.
  ,,   Hanna, d. of Thomas &   Edwards.
16$\frac{5}{6}\frac{9}{0}$, Jan. 7. [torn] of John & Margaret Cox, Taylor.
  ,,   [torn] d. of Francis & Elizabeth Hawkes.
  ,, Jan. 28. [torn] of William & Lowre Bird, Carpenter.
  ,,   [torn] of Thomas Mayo.
  ,, Feb. 13. [torn] d. of Mr. Richard Carelesse.
  ,, Mar. 23. [torn] d. of Richard & Alse Atkisse, Naylor.
  ,, [omitted]. John, s. of Nicholas Wyley, Naylor.

MARRIAGES.

1654, [torn out]. John, s. of Randulf Robinson, of Bartumney,
                   in Chesheare, husbandman, and Mary, d.
                   of Francis Penne, B. ; before Sir John
                   Wyrley.

  ,, Sept. 5. Thomas, s. of Raphe Kendricke, of [torn out],
                 Co. Stafford, and Mary, d. of Walter Hart
                 (weaver), of Uper Penne, Co. Stafford, B. ;
                 before Sir John Wyrley.

  ,, Oct. 17. John Bird, Naylor, and Anne, d. of Richard
                Parkhouse, of Wednesbury, dec., B. ;
                before Sir J. Wyrley.

  ,, Oct. 26. John Cartwright, Naylor, and Alse, d. of
                Henry Hunt, Skiner, of Birmingham, Co.
                Warwick, B. ; before Sir John Wyrley.

  ,, Nov. 1. [torn out], Naylor, and Annis, d. of Edward
                Cole, Naylor, dec., B. ; before Sir John
                Wyrley.

ov. 7. [*torn out*], s. of Christopher Okeley, and Joyce,
d. of Ambrose Underhill, of Worley
Wigorne, Co. Salop, B. ; before Sir John
Wyrley.

ov. 21. Edward Riley, Naylor, and Margery, d. of
Richard Ashmore, Naylor, dec., B. ;
before Sir John Wyrley.

ec. 4. John, s. of Thomas Reeves, Blacksmith, and
Margaret, d. of Thomas Shortus, of
Wednesbury, B. ; before Sir John Wyrley.

ec. 26. Raphe, s. of Richard Gretton, Glover, and
Mary, d. of Roger Hill, furnasseman, of
Dudley, dec., B. ; before Sir John
Wyrley.

ay 3. Raphe Culwicke, Bucklemaker, s. of William
Culwicke, husbandman, of the Cline, in
the parish of Pattingam, Co. Stafford,
dec., and Elizabeth, d. of William Frith,
Taylor.

ay 29. Roger Southall & Eleanor, d. of Edward
Morris, B. ; John Wyrley.

ly 4. William, s. of Henry Juger, Naylor, and
Anne, d. of Thomas Atkisse, Naylor, B. ;
before Mr. Henry Stone.

ly 9. John, s. of Alexander Lowe, Ironmonger,
and Prissilla, d. of Mr. William Robins,
late of Bilson, Co. Stafford, dec., B. ;
before Mr. Henry Stone.

t. 24. Thomas Mayou, Lawrimer, s. of John Mayou,
of Aldridge, Husbandman, and Isabell, d.
of Thomas Renalls, Weaver, dec., B. ;
before Sir John Wyrley.

t. 30. Richard, s. of Richard Wright, Naylor, and
Alse, d. of Thomas Grey, Husbandman,
of Tippon, Co. Stafford, dec., B. ; before
Mr. William Smith, Mayor of Walsall.

c. 18. William Nighingall, Naylor, of Tippon, and
Elizabeth, d. of Francis Hawkes, Naylor,
dec., B. ; before Mr. Henry Stone.

1655, Dec. 24. Edward, s. of Richard **Dix**, Husbandman, of
                Sutton Colefield, and Ellenor Wall, wid-
                dowe, B. ; before Sir John Wyrley.

,, Dec. 24.   Edward Hawkes, Naylor, and Anne Howes,
               widdowe, B. ; before Sir John Wyrley.

165⅚, Feb. 11. Joseph Broome, Naylor, s. of John Broome,
               husbandman, of Tadstone, Co. Hereford,
               and Margery, d. of William Hadley,
               Naylor, dec., B. ; before Sir John Wyrley,
               at West Bromwich.

,, Feb. 25.   Richard, s. of Richard Atkisse, Naylor, and
               Margaret, d. of John Westwood, Naylor,
               B. ; before Sir John Wyrley.

,, Mar. 11.   Francis, s. of Francis Hawkes, Naylor, and
               Elizabeth, d. of John Jevon, yeoman, of
               Tippon, B. ; before Mr. Henry Stone.

,, Mar. 17.   Alexander, s. of Henry Teea, Naylor, and
               Ellenor Yardley, widdowe, B. ; before
               Sir John Wyrley.

,, Mar. 24.   Henry, s. of Francis Penn, Naylor, dec., and
               Mary, d. of Randall Robinson, husband-
               man, of Bartumney, Co. Chester, B. ;
               before Mr. George Hill, of Walsall, Justice
               of the Peace.

,, Mar. 31.   Joseph, s. of Raphe Morris, bucklemaker,
               and Hanna, d. of George Lee, husband-
               man, of Tippon, B. ; before Mr. Henry
               Stone.

1656, Apr. 22. Nicholas, s. of John Wiley, naylor, and Joane
               Hadley, Mayden, d. of William Hadey
               (*sic.*), naylor, dec., B. ; before Sir John
               Wyrley·

,, May 27.   John, s. of Richard Gretton, glover, and
               Joane, d. of Francis Wiley, naylor, B. ;
               before Sir John Wyrley, at Hampstede Hall.

,, May 27.   Raphe Wotton, husbandman, and Elizabeth
               Morris, of Yardley, Co. Worcester, wid-
               dowe, B. ; before Sir John Wyrley, **at**
               Hampstede.

1656, June 3. Walter, s. of Walter Steevens, bucklemaker,
and Elizabeth, d. of Oliver Whitehouse,
of Wednesbury, naylor, B. ; before Mr.
William Smith, Mayor of Walsall.

„ Aug. 27. Raphell Avory, servant to Mr. Thomas Foley,
and Margaret, d. of John Elton, of Walsall,
weaver, B. ; before Sir John Wyrley.

„ Oct. 14. John, s. of John Cumberbess, of Birmingham,
glover, and Joyce Watson, of Hands-
worth, B. ; before Sir John Wyrley.

„ Oct. 18. Humphrey Case, naylor, s. of [*omitted*] Case,
gardner, and Elizabeth, d. of William
Turton, naylor, B. ; before Sir John
Wyrley.

„ Nov. 11. William Smith, bucklemaker, and Anne, d.
of John Aughton, blacksmith, B. ; before
Mr. Henry Stone.

165 6/7, Feb. 3. Ambrose Cooper, spurrier & gunsmith, s. of
Ambrose Cooper, of Castle Bromwich, Co.
Warwicke, tirritmaker, and Jane, d. of
William Spooner, of Barre, husbandman,
B. ; before Sir John Wyrley.

1657, Apr. 6. Nicholas Rider, miller, and Elizabeth, d. of
Vincent (?) Eayles, of Castle Bromwich,
Co. Warwicke, husbandman, B. ; before
Sir John Wyrley.

„ May 12. John, s. of Henry Edwards, naylor, and
Anne, d. of William Turton, naylor, B. ;
before Sir John Wyrley.

„ May 13. William Johnson, s. of Francis Jonson, and
Elizabeth, d. of William Partridge, bucklemaker, B. ; before Sir John Wyrley.

„ June 9. John, s. of Edward Taylor, naylor, of Wednes-
bury, dec., and Elizabeth, d. of William
Bird, carpenter, dec., B. ; before Mr.
Henry Stone.

„ June 24. Francis Poultney, husbandman, and Elizabeth, d. of Thomas Kerby, miller, dec.,
B. ; before Mr. William Smith.

1657, July   7.   John Woodward, of Hales-owen, naylor, s. of Richard Woodward, naylor, and Katharine, d. of John Aughton, blacksmith, B. ; before Mr. Henry Stone.

"   Sept. 21.   Joseph, s. of William Johnson, naylor, and Elizabeth, d. of Gregory Woodward, locksmith, B. ; before Sir John Wyrley.

"   Oct. 20.   John, s. of William Hadley, naylor, and Jane Gobbins, of Tettenhall, Co. of Stafford, B. ; by Mr. Hilton, our Minister.

"   Dec.   1.   Edward, s. of Edward Tranter, naylor, and Margery Riley, widdowe, B. ; by Mr. Hilton, our Minister.

"   Dec.   5.   Henry, s. of Henry Frieth, naylor, and Anne, d. of Henry Smith, bucklemaker, of Walsall, B. ; by Mr. Hilton, our Minister.

"   Dec.   8.   William Meares, naylor, and Sarah, d. of George Lee, of Tippon, husbandman, B. by Mr. Hilton, our Minister.

165⅞, Feb. 28.   Thomas Culwicke, naylor, and Sarah, d. of Thomas Litham, naylor, B. ; by Mr. Hilton, our Minister.

1658, June   1.   William Steevens, naylor, and Frances, d. of Richard Dudley, naylor, dec., B. ; by Mr. Hilton, our Minister.

"   June   1.   Thomas, s. of Henry Frith, naylor, and Anne, d. of George Underhill, weaver, dec., B. ; by Mr. Hilton, our Minister.

"   June 22.   Richard Shinton, naylor, and Mary, d. of John Stamps, husbandman, dec., B. ; by Mr. Hilton, our Minister.

"   Sept. 16.   Roger Evans and Anne, d. of Edward Grey, husbandman, of Bilson, B. ; by Mr. Hilton, our Minister.

"   Nov. 23.   John Baker, yeoman, of Sillill, Co. of Warwick, and Anne, d. of William Ward, husbandman, M. ; by our Minister, Mr. Richard Hilton.

1659, June 10.   Thomas France, of the Forge, and Hanna   /
                 Brookes, of Birmingham, M. ; by our
                 Minister, Mr. Richard Hilton.

„ July 12.   Mr. William Turton, Minister of Rowley, and
                 Mrs. Margery Groue, M. ; by our Minister,
                 Mr. Richard Hilton.

BURIALLS. 1653.

1653, Oct.   31.   William Jones, Naylor.

„ Dec.   13.   William Hadley, Naylor.

165¾, Jan.   24.   Jean Orris, Wid.

„ Jan.   27.   Thomas, s. of Robert Jones, Naylor.

„ Jan.   30.   Joyce Frith, Wid.

„ Feb.   28.   William Liddiatt, Naylor.

„ Mar.   1.   Abigall, d. of John Walker, Bucklemaker.

„ Mar.   7.   Thomas, s. of Thomas Atkisse, Naylor.

„ Mar.   10.   Mary, d. of Edward Hodgkins, Naylor.

„ Mar.   11.   Thomas, s. of Thomas Brisco, Naylor.

1654, Mar.   25.   Robert Curtlor, Yeoman.

„ Mar.   27.   Elizabeth, d. of John Parkes, lab.

„ Apr.   2.   John, s. of John Yardley, Naylor.

„ Apr.   3.   Mary, d. of Edward Burges, Naylor.

„ Apr.   25.   Mary, d. of Robert Bate, Naylor.

„ Apr.   27.   Elizabeth, d. of Mr. John Shilton, Esq.

„ May   26.   Anne, d. of William Partridge, bucklemaker.

„ May   29.   William, s. of Thomas Morris, Blacksmith.

„ June   6.   Hanna, d. of Edward Dudley, Cooper.

„ July   8.   [*omitted*], w. of John Bird, Naylor.

„ July   23.   Ellenor, w. of William Partridge, Buckle-
             maker.

„ July   26.   William Osbourne, Naylor, the Par. Clarke.

„ Aug.   8.   Samuell, s. of Thomas Jesson, Yeoman.

„ Aug.   31.   Raphe Heywood, Weaver.

„ Oct.   10.   Elizabeth, d. of Michaell Simcox.

„ Oct.   15.   William, s. of John Fenton, Naylor.

„ Nov.   14.   Elizabeth, d. of Henry Avery.

„ Nov.   15.   Joane Bull, wid.

„ Nov.   19.   Mary, d. of Thomas Hadley, Naylor.

1654, Nov. 20.	Ellenor, w. of Richard Litham.
,, [*torn.*]	Anne Coling, of Barre.
,, [*torn.*]	Margaret, d. of Roland Bett, Naylor.
,, [*torn.*]	Stokes, Naylor.
,, [*torn.*]	Naylor, A daughter.
,, [*torn.*]	Elizabeth, w. of Raphe Watton, Lab.
,, [*torn.*] 17.	wid.
,, [*torn.*]	's. of Wm.
1655, Apr. 20.	Mary, d. of John [*torn out*], Naylor.
,, Apr. 26.	Thomas Read, Warrener.
,, Apr. 26.	Christopher, s. of Thomas [*torn out*], of Bar.
,, Apr. 30.	Edward, Cotterell, a Beyger.
,, May 2.	Francis Penne, Naylor.
,, May 5.	John, s. of John Preston.
,, May 11.	Raphe Stanley, Naylor.
,, June 22.	John Preston, Naylor.
,, June 23.	Alexander Jarvis, yeoman.
,, June 23.	Samuell, s. of Roger Griffith, Sawyer.
,, June 25.	Robert, s. of Robert Turner, weaver.
,, July 15.	George Bird, Naylor.
,, July 18.	William, s. of Raphe Kendricke, Naylor.
,, July 27.	Anne, w. of Gregory Woodward.
,, Aug. 1.	Thomas Reeves, of Barre.
,, Sept. 23.	William Partridge, Bucklemaker.
,, Oct. 11.	Robert Vamos, of Wednesbury, fardyman.
,, Nov. 6.	Edward, s. of Edward Morris.
,, Nov. 8.	Emm, w. of Thomas Cup, weaver.
,, Nov. 21.	Edward Dudley, Butcher.
,, Nov. 21.	Richard, s. of Richard Parkes, Naylor.
√ 165⅚, Jan. 23.	Elizabeth Hall, wid.
,, Jan. 28.	Ely Roberts, a child still borne.
,, Feb. 1.	Master William Turton, of the Mill.
,, Feb. 7.	Frances, d. of William Liddiatt.
,, Mar. 4.	Ellenor, d. of Francis Tomkinson.
1656, Apr. 14.	William, s. of Richard Sterry.
,, Apr. 17.	Appelle, d. of Edward Hill, Naylor.
,, Apr. 23.	Thomas, s. of Edward Hill, Naylor.
,, Apr. 30.	Sarah, d. of Mr. William Turton.
,, June 13.	w, of John Meanley, of Barre.

1656,	June	28.	Anne, d. of John Meanley, of Barre.
,,	June	28.	s. of Robert Merehurst.
,,	July	16.	d. of George Marsh.
,,	July	22.	of Henry Teda.
,,	July	23.	of Mr. William Turton.
,,	July	23.	
,,	July	30.	
,,	Sept.		Thomas Mayou, unbaptized.
,,	Sept.		William Partridge, a child still borne.
,,	Sept.	19.	Mary, d. of Simcox.
,,	Oct.	15.	John, s. of Mr. William Turton.
√ ,,	Oct.	26.	Edward, s. of Richard Brookes.
,,	Oct.	27.	Joseph Broom, still borne.
,,	Nov.	9.	Thomas [*torn*], Joyner, a child unbap.
,,	Nov.	12.	William, s. of William Osborne, Naylor.
,,	Nov.	28.	Roger Chetwin, Naylor.
,,	Dec.	7.	Mary, w. of John Bird, Carpenter.
,,	Dec.	8.	William, s. of William Bird, Naylor.
,,	Dec.	16.	Elizabeth, d. of John Jones, Naylor.
,,	Dec.	19.	Ellenor, d. of Thomas Bird, Joyner.
165⁶⁄₇,	Jan.	5.	Ann, d. of John Round, of Asbury.
,,	Jan.	14.	Wid. Johnson.
,,	Mar.	3.	Thomas Gretton, hbdman.
,,	Mar.	15.	Francis, s. of Francis Hawkes.
,,	Mar.	23.	Margaret Dutton, wid.
1657,	Mar.	30.	The wife of Edward Fenton.
,,	Apr.	4.	William Rowith, Apprentice to Richard Parkes.
,,	Apr.	5.	Alse Swindells, a stranger.
,,	Apr.	10.	Richard, s. of John Boyer.
,,	Apr.	11.	Ellenor Dudley, wid.
,,	Apr.	24.	Judith, d. of John Ward, Naylor.
,,	June	7.	Elizabeth Wiersdale, wid.
,,	June	11.	Wm. Taylor had an infant unbap.
,,	June	22.	Raphe Kendrick had a child still born.
,,	July	2.	Katharine Cole, wid.
,,	July	5.	Thomas Cox, weaver.
,,	July	31.	Paull, s. of John Edwards, Naylor.
,,	Aug.	15.	Ellenor, d. of Richard James, hbdman.

1657, Sept. 1.   Jone Woodward, wid.
  ,, Sept. 5.   Roger Osburne, Bellowesmaker.
  ,, Sept. 16. Humfrey Case had a child unbap.
  ,, Sept. 26.   Liddiat.
                  Richard Meare, of Morton.
                     w. of Mr. Edward Grene.

  ,, Nov. 16.
  ,, Nov. 30. George Kendrick.
  ,, Dec. 15. John, s. of Richard
  ,, Dec. 16. Francis Greene.
  ,, Dec. 20. Richard Tranter, Naylor.
165⅞, Jan. 11. Nicholas, s. of William Preston.
  ,, Jan. 13. Henry Penne had a child born & bur.
  ,, Jan. 16. George Robiler, of Sobury.
  ,, Jan. 20.   w, of Mathew Perry.
  ,, Feb. 4.   John, s. of John Gretton.
  ,, Feb. 5.   William Cox.
  ,, Feb. 8.   Margery Wiley, wid.
  ,, Mar. 2.   Mary Tranter, wid.
  ,, Mar. 22. Elizabeth France, wid.
1658, Apr. 10. The w. of Edward Morris.
  ,, Apr. 23. John Stamps.
  ,, Apr. 24. Margaret Bird, wid.
  ,, Apr. 25. Sarah, d. of Francis Liddiatt.
  ,, Apr. 26. William Dugar.
  ,, Apr. 26. Ellenor, d. of Francis Liddiatt.
  ,, Apr. 27. Richard, s. of John Bird, Naylor.
  ,, June 17. Edward Tull, Naylor.
  ,, June 22. John Browne, a servant at the Swanne.
  ,, Aug. 5.   Mrs. Field Whorwood.
  ,, Aug. 6.   Elizabeth, w. of Nicholas Okely.
  ,, Aug. 7.   Ellenor, w. of John Parkes, Musitian.
  ,, Aug. 13. Robert Jones.
  ,, Aug. 20. George Simcox.
  ,, Aug. 24. [*omitted*] of Roger Griffin.
  ,, Sept. 1. Roger Collings.
  ,, Sept. 6. Philip France.
  ,, Sept. 18. Margery Carelesse, wid.
  ,, Sept. 18. Richard Dudley.

1658, Sept. 21.   Robert Turner, Naylor.
   ,,   Oct.   2.   William Keeling, of Oldbury.
   ,,   Oct. 10.   Francis, s. of Francis Liddiatt.
   ,,   Oct. 19.   Lowe.
   ,,   Oct. 22.   w. of Edward Tranter.
   ,,   Oct. 27.   Naylor.
   ,,   Oct. 30.   John Baylie, Carpenter.
   ,,   Nov. 20.   w. of William Reding.
   ,,   Nov. 30.   of William
   ,,   Dec.   6.
   ,,   Dec. 29.

CPSIA information can be obtained
at www.ICGtesting.com
Printed in the USA
BVHW04*1238140918
527538BV00007B/448/P